# PLAYING AROUND ARISTOPHANES

*Essays in celebration of the completion of the edition*
*of the Comedies of Aristophanes*
*by*

ALAN SOMMERSTEIN

Edited by

LYNN KOZAK AND JOHN RICH

Aris & Phillips is an imprint of
Oxbow Books, Park End Place, Oxford OX1 1HN

ISBN  978-0-85668-771-6     0-85668-771-5

A CIP record for this book is available from the British Library

Printed in the United Kingdom
at the University Press,
Cambridge

# Contents

# Preface

Alan Sommerstein joined the staff of the University of Nottingham in 1974 and has continued there to this day, as successively Lecturer, Reader, and (from 1988) Professor of Greek. During this period he has produced a stream of distinguished books, editions and articles on many aspects of Greek drama and society. Among all these, one work stands out: the complete edition of the plays of Aristophanes in twelve volumes (one for each play, followed by an index volume), of which the first appeared in 1980 and the last early in 2003 (2002 on the title-page). This edition has been universally admired for the vividness and accuracy of the translation, the lucidity and accessibility of the exposition, and the high quality of the scholarship, and has achieved the classic status for today's readers which that of Benjamin Bickley Rogers held a century earlier.

My colleagues and I in the Nottingham Department of Classics felt that we should not allow to go unmarked the completion of this great edition, the most remarkable achievement in classical studies to have been produced by any member of the University. A celebratory colloquium was accordingly held on 14 May 2003, under the title *Playing around Aristophanes*. The present volume incorporates revised versions of all but one of the papers delivered on that occasion, along with two additional papers, namely the contribution by Bernhard Zimmermann, who was unable to be present at the conference, and Alan Sommerstein's delightful memoir.

We were pleased that David Brown of Oxbow Books, who took over the Aris & Phillips imprint on the retirement of Adrian Phillips in 2002, was able to attend the colloquium, and are grateful to him and his colleagues, especially Clare Litt and Val Lamb, for their work in bringing the volume to publication. We also thank the University of Nottingham for a generous grant towards the colloquium costs. Various Nottingham colleagues gave valuable assistance in the production of both the colloquium and the book. Two deserve special thanks. Alan's graduate student and my co-editor, Lynn Kozak, has carried out the bulk of the editorial work with admirable care and cheerfulness. Alan Sommerstein himself has helped in innumerable ways throughout the process, always with his customary skill and despatch, notably in translating Prof. Zimmermann's contribution and reading through the proofs.

*Nottingham*                                                                      JWR
*March 2005*

# Poetics and politics in the comedies of Aristophanes

## *Bernhard Zimmermann*

*(*Albert-Ludwigs-Universität, Freiburg)

## I

If one glances at a reference book on ancient Graeco-Roman literature, one usually finds in the entry on Aristophanes the statement, expressed in various ways which amount to much the same thing, that Aristophanic comedy, especially in the fifth century BC, is "political". This is undoubtedly correct, but it requires some modification and explanation, since the label "political" could mislead the naïve reader. In the interpretation of Greek dramas of the fifth century, not only comedies but also tragedies and satyr-plays, the term "political" should not be understood in the restricted modern sense of "relating to politics". The meaning of "political" in the fifth century is that the author has made all the affairs of the *polis* – the city of Athens – or at least those which he saw as important, part of the content of his plays (the question of his aims in doing so is of course one of the most discussed and most controversial issues in the study both of tragedy and particularly of comedy). Some crucial concerns of the *polis*, to be sure, are also thoroughly political issues in the modern sense – war and peace, the behaviour of politicians and of the military élite (in Athens these were usually the same persons), the bribery and corruption of voters, to name only a few topics. But religion, culture, and education (*paideia*) in the widest sense, were also "political" in the sense of being matters of concern to the *polis*; and so especially were the poetic genres that represented the basis of the *paideia* of the *polis*, namely tragedy and dithyramb. Thus not only Aristophanes but also his contemporaries such as Cratinus, Eupolis and Pherecrates (to name only a few of the leading figures) place themselves in a relationship with the sister genre of tragedy and with the choral lyric genre of dithyramb – the two genres which were performed at the same Dionysiac festival, the Great Dionysia – which is one of parodic critique but at the same time also of literary criticism.[1] In addition to aspects of the language and content of the works they parody, it is above all their musical side to which the comic dramatists direct their attention and which is taken as an indication of the mentality of the poet concerned.[2] However, issues relating to education more generally, from the teaching of music and poetry to children up to rhetorical and philosophical study, also figure among the regular themes of comedy, and the specialized sciences of the time – such as medicine, mathematics, astronomy, grammar and even town planning – receive attention, again for the most part of a parodic kind.[3]

The various parodies and critical analyses of particular specialities that Aristophanes undertakes naturally serve in the first place to further the basic aim of comedy – to arouse laughter at the expense of the persons and things parodied. In addition, though, in the uncovering of abuses and the exposure of those responsible for them, who are identified and mocked by name (*onomasti komodein*), he offers enlightening social analyses: the eyes of the audience are opened, their attention is drawn to their weak spots and above all to those who understand how to exploit those weak spots. Aristophanes (to be precise, the chorus in his name) makes this claim in the very first surviving comedy, *Acharnians* (633–5):

φησὶν δ' εἶναι πολλῶν ἀγαθῶν ἄξιος ὑμῖν ὁ ποιητής,
παύσας ὑμᾶς ξενικοῖσι λόγοις μὴ λίαν ἐξαπατᾶσθαι,
μηδ' ἥδεσθαι θωπευομένους, μηδ' εἶναι χαυνοπολίτας.

Our poet says that he deserves a rich reward at your hands for having stopped you being too easily deceived by the words of foreigners, taking pleasure in flattery, being citizens of Emptyhead.[4]

---

[1] On comic parody of tragedy and dithyramb see respectively Rau 1967 and Zimmermann 1997.

[2] Particularly relevant is a fragment of Pherecrates (fr. 155 K-A), in which the personification of Music complains of the ill-treatment she has received from the musical innovators of the late fifth century; cf. Zimmermann 1992b.

[3] Medicine: Zimmermann 1992b. Town planning: Zimmermann 1993 and more recently (covering the comic fragments also) Imperio 1998: 43ff.

[4] Translations, here and subsequently, are taken from Sommerstein 1980 *et seqq*.

In the centre of this effort at enlightenment pursued in Aristophanic comedy stands above all, in the plays produced after the Sicilian Expedition, the question how it could happen that Athens, after the *polis* had repelled the gigantic Persian superpower and then brought her own power to its peak, could have sunk so low that it now had to fight for its very survival in a war of nearly thirty years with Sparta. Aristophanes (more precisely, the chorus of initiates in the parabasis of *Frogs* [686–705, 718–37]) sees the cause as being the fragmentation of society into separate, competing and conflicting interest-groups, the *hetaireiai*, which sacrificed the only effective foundation of the *polis*, namely unity (*homónoia*), to their selfish group interests.

## II

Aristophanes parodies and analyses tragedy and dithyramb, though sometimes, in doing so, he sketches out a prescriptive poetics of the two sister genres; he also, especially in his parabases, has things to say about his own genre, and in saying them puts forward both poetic and political norms by which a good comic poet should be guided.

> μή μοι φθονήσητ᾽, ἄνδρες οἱ θεώμενοι,
> εἰ πτωχὸς ὢν ἔπειτ᾽ ἐν Ἀθηναίοις λέγειν
> μέλλω περὶ τῆς πόλεως, τρυγῳδίαν ποιῶν.
> τὸ γὰρ δίκαιον οἶδε καὶ τρυγῳδία·
> ἐγὼ δὲ λέξω δεινὰ μέν, δίκαια δέ.

> Be not indignant with me, members of the audience, if, though a beggar, I speak before the Athenians about public affairs in a comedy. Even comedy is acquainted with justice; and what I have to say will be shocking, but it will be right. (*Ach.* 497–501)

With the neologism *trygodia* "comedy", formed on the model of *tragodia* "tragedy", and with the particle *kai* "even", Aristophanes through the mouth of Dicaeopolis[5] points out that comedy *too* can have what tragedy

---

[5] For the identification of Aristophanes and Dicaeopolis cf. Sommerstein 1980: 180 (on 500).

was expected to have, a serious aim and an educative function.[6] On the basis of democratic free speech (*parrhesia*) the poet makes the claim that he and his genre have the right to express to his fellow-citizens opinions that may be uncongenial, to open their eyes, and thereby also to show citizens of other *poleis* attending the performances the nature of life in a democratic *polis* organized on the Athenian pattern.

Aristophanes derives his justification for the freedom of speech he exercises in comedy from comedy's Dionysiac roots, since by ancient custom the right to mock individuals by name was attached to the Dionysiac mysteries (*Frogs* 368). The chorus of mystic initiates in *Frogs* is the appropriate group to give, at the end of the fifth-century phase of Old Comedy, a definition of this cultically sanctioned freedom to mock as an essential element of the content of the genre (*Frogs* 391–5, 405–10). It is permitted to Dionysus' sacred festival chorus to jest and mock as it dances (*Frogs* 375f., 390, 394, 409). But jesting and mockery are not ends in themselves: they are achieved with material that has serious content (*Frogs* 391f.). With this Aristophanic comedy goes beyond the purely cultic framework to become a *polis* genre with a function in the community that is not solely linked to the festival: to perform a work of enlightenment and to serve the public by opening its eyes. "It is right and proper", sing the chorus of initiates in the parabasis of *Frogs* (686f.), "for the sacred chorus to take part in giving good advice and instruction to the community", and with this they open the crucial theme of the agon between Euripides and Aeschylus – the didactic function of the *polis*-oriented poetic genres.

To do justice to this role of his in the *polis*, the poet must – banal as this may sound – write plays that appeal to his audience. In the parabases of his plays from the time of the Archidamian War, Aristophanes is continually reflecting on this fundamental prerequisite. What must a comedy be like, if it is both to be of high quality and to win public approval? And what must an audience be like, if it is to be able to judge the quality of a play?

---

[6] Cf. Olson 2002: 201 (on 500). The didactic function of tragedy, and of poetry in general, is expounded in the agon of *Frogs* (1030–6). While the Aristophanic Aeschylus emphasizes that his plays he presents models of civic virtue (1013–29) and keeps what is shameful off the stage (1053–5), the Aristophanic Euripides sees his function as being to educate the citizenry in analytical thought and rhetorical skills (971–9).

In brief summary, one can extract from the comedies the following "poetics" and the following model of the interaction between the comic text and its audience. It is, to be sure, the claim of every comic poet to be offering his audience something new (*Clouds* 547, *Wasps* 1044). For Aristophanes, however, there are limits, set by good taste (*Peace* 739–51, *Frogs* 1–34) and by the principle of moderation (*sophrosýne, Clouds* 537, *Wasps* 1023–8), so that he can proudly claim for his comic art the epithet "urban(e)" (*asteíos, Frogs* 901, 906; *ouk agoraíos, Peace* 750). With similar pride he emphasizes that a good comedy should rely solely on its literary quality (*Peace* 749f). Such a comedy can only be successful if it encounters an audience which shares the poet's criteria of quality and which is equally *sophós* and *dexiós* (*Clouds* 518–32, *Wasps* 1051–9).[7] If that is not the case, even the best poet with the best comedy can come to grief, as Aristophanes did with *Clouds*. If one combines the characterisations that Aristophanes gives of the poets who figure in his short history of Attic comedy (*Knights* 520–40), one can put together from the separate elements there presented the ideal form of comedy against which Aristophanes wants to have himself measured. In the musical field, this comprises musical richness and daring mimetic play in music and song, for which Magnes serves as the model (*Knights* 520–5), paired with "native Dionysiac power" in the lyrics (Cratinus, 526–30); above all, though, there must be clever ideas, brought on stage without great expense and with sober intelligence (Crates, 537–40). Since none of these three poets enjoyed enduring success, despite their excellence in one respect or another, it follows that a really good, successful poet must combine in himself the properties of all the three models. It is evident that Aristophanes sets the greatest value on the properties ascribed to Crates, whom he has placed, contrary to chronology, last of the trio.

If against this background, and with Crates as our measuring rod – the poet who according to Aristotle (*Poetics* 1449b7–9) "was the first Athenian comic dramatist to break away from the 'iambic style' (i.e. from satire and invective) and write plays on 'universal' rather than topical or

---

[7] On these concepts cf. Dover 1992: 8f., Dover 1993: 14.

parochial themes"[8] – we compare Aristophanic comedy with the tragedy of the same period, then on reducing Aristophanes' comedies to their *mythos* in the sense of Aristotle's *Poetics* (1450a15) – that is, to the basic structure of events that constitutes the action (σύστασις τῶν πραγμάτων) – what strikes the eye is more the common features of the two genres than their differences. The tragic poetry of an Aeschylus, a Sophocles or a Euripides continually reflects, through the mirror of myth, contemporary problems of social existence; but these same problems find in comedy a jovial, burlesque, parodic and critical, sometimes grotesque and obscene, representation in the guise of a comically exaggerated, unreal, fantastical topicality, so that in full agreement with the Aristophanes of Plato's *Symposium*[9] the two genres, tragedy and comedy, must be treated as forms of expression that significantly complement each other. The opposition of war and peace, with all its consequences for society, the family and the individual, is a theme running right through fifth-century tragedy as much as fifth-century comedy; I need mention only the *Seven against Thebes* and *Oresteia* of Aeschylus, the *Hecuba* and *Trojan Women* of Euripides on one side, or the *Acharnians, Peace* and *Lysistrata* of Aristophanes on the other. The relationship of the sexes is central to both genres: think of Agamemnon and Clytaemestra in Aeschylus' *Agamemnon*, Alcestis and Admetus in Euripides' *Alcestis*, Medea and Jason in his *Medea*, Hippolytus and Phaedra in his *Hippolytus*, or of Ajax and Tecmessa in Sophocles' *Ajax* and of Heracles and Deianeira in his *Trachiniae*. In Aristophanes' *Lysistrata* and *Ecclesiazusae* the relationship, or rather the conflict, of the sexes is made the theme of the comedy; in the marriage of Trygaeus ("the Vintager") and Opora ("the Vintage") in *Peace* the relationship, the union, of man and wife becomes the scenic symbol for peace, for the return of the peasants to the countryside which is bound up with the conclusion of peace, for sowing and ingathering in a rural idyll.

The relationship between current reality, the world in which the spectators live, and the action on stage, is established in different ways in the two genres of comedy and tragedy. In tragedy the connection to the present day is established through "bridges", through concepts or ideas

---

[8] Sommerstein 1981: 172f.; on the poetics implicit in Aristophanes' treatment of his predecessors, cf. Sommerstein 1992.

[9] 189c2–d2, cf. Dover 1980:112 ff.

from current discourse, which pull the mythical action towards the here-and-now of the spectator.[10] The tension between current problems and stage action, the oscillation between the two poles of myth and the here-and-now,[11] which is secured by these bridges, can (but need not) trigger reflection in the spectator, can bring him to interpret his situation as a *polis* citizen against the foil of the tragic action.[12]

Comedy pursues the opposite route to that taken by its sister genre. It starts from the present, from an unsatisfactory state of affairs at the time of production, from which it fashions its *kritische Idee* and develops its *komische Thema*.[13] To arouse reflection in the spectator, however, comedy also needs a distancing between the stage action and the world in which the audience lives, and it achieves this through precisely what Bertolt Brecht called *Verfremdung*: through displacement into utopian spaces,[14] or through fantasy devices such as the wine of peace in *Acharnians* or the ride on the dung-beetle in *Peace*, or through the reversal of normal relationships (what scholars like to label "carnivalesque" reversals), as of the relationship of old and young in *Wasps* or of the sexes in *Lysistrata* and *Ecclesiazusae*. The bridges between reality and the theatrical world of

---

[10] The classic instance is the institution of the Areopagus in Aeschylus' *Eumenides*, in which, by a technique similar to that of choral lyric, a recent event, the reform of Ephialtes, is aetiologically anchored in the mythical history of the city of Athens; cf. Sommerstein 1989: 25–32. In Euripides' *Orestes* the use of a word (*hetairía*: 804, 1072, 1079) originating from the political discourse of the time of production (408) places the stage action in direct connection with political events in Athens after the oligarchic coup of 411; cf. Zimmermann 2000: 132–5.

[11] Sourvinou-Inwood 1989: 36 speaks of "distancing devices" which *separate* the action from the world of the spectator, and of "zooming devices" which bring it *towards* the present day. On this cf. also Grethlein 2003: 34–43.

[12] In making such an interpretation the spectator is naturally offered assistance above all in the choral songs of tragedy, which transcend the actual stage action and thereby stimulate reflection – in full agreement with Friedrich Schiller's view of the role of the chorus in drama (*Über den Gebrauch des Chors in der Tragödie*, Preface to *Die Braut von Messina*).

[13] For the terminology cf. Koch 1968. On the "ideal" plot structure of Old Comedy, cf. Zimmermann 1998: 35–44.

[14] Cf. Zimmermann 1983.

comic fantasy, between the *polis* of Athens and "Aristophanopolis",[15] are established by means of the many topical references – though these decline in the course of Aristophanes' career from *Acharnians* to *Wealth* in favour of a greater generality and timelessness – and especially through *onomasti komodein*, the mockery by name of individuals known to the whole city.

# III

This, the most notable distinctive feature of Old Comedy, mockery by name, which (together with formal differences due to the presence of a chorus) distinguishes the comedy of the fifth century from that of the fourth century and the Hellenistic period, forms the best basis for the exposition of one of the most extensively discussed and most intensely controversial questions in the study of comedy: the question of the political function of Aristophanic comedy.[16] The formation of modern theories was preceded, in just this field, by an expression of opinion by a contemporary: the statement of a man of sharp tongue and acute intelligence, the anonymous author of the pamphlet *On the Athenian State*, which must have been produced in the period of Aristophanes' earliest comedies, in all probability before 424. The Old Oligarch explains *onomasti komodein* as an excellent device for political argument in Athenian society at the time of the Archidamian War (2.18):

> "They [i.e. the common people] do not allow the *demos* [as a whole] to be mocked or spoken ill of, in order that their own reputation should not be damaged. In the case of individuals, on the other hand, they encourage anyone who wishes to do so, since they know well that the victim of mockery does not as a rule belong to the *demos* or to the masses, but is either rich, or of high birth, or influential. Only a few of the poor and common people are mocked, and these only if they meddle too much in other people's affairs and try [to gain privileges and] to have more than

---

[15] A neologism based on A.S. Gratwick's neat and pertinent coinage "Plautopolis" (Gratwick 1993: 15).

[16] I deliberately say "Aristophanic", because any attempt to determine the functions of comedy in the hands of other fifth-century authors would have to be preceded by a thorough examination of their fragments. On personal jokes, cf. Sommerstein 1996b.

the *demos*, so that in the case of men of that kind too they do not feel aggrieved at their being mocked."

The author ascribes a double function to the mockery of well-known contemporaries by name. On the one hand the *demos*, through personal mockery, is marking as outsiders certain individuals who stand out as distinct from the mass of Athenians by particular attributes: wealth, noble birth, or some particular *dýnamis* (ability), be this intellectual or political. On the other hand the *demos* leaves open to mockery all those who, while they may come from its own ranks and be members of "the people", stand out from the group by their behaviour or their abilities and deliberately try to separate themselves from the rest of their class. The *demos* itself,[17] by contrast, is exempt from mockery; it is the measure of all things; it not only determines what the law is in Athens (1.18) but also lays down the criteria that determine exclusion and inclusion.

In what follows I will examine some examples of the exclusory function of mockery, which the Old Oligarch highlights as an essential feature of fifth-century comedy. In *Acharnians* the chorus takes the successes of the comic hero Dicaeopolis, especially the way he brusquely gets rid of all intruders and favour-seekers, as an occasion to imagine what other figures in public life Dicaeopolis could easily remove from the sphere in which he moves. According to the chorus's wish-fulfilling imaginings, Dicaeopolis will indiscriminately and without difficulty chase away people such as the sycophant Ctesias and other members of his profession,[18] the second-rank politician Hyperbolus, the comic poet Cratinus, the proverbially cowardly Cleonymus (cf. *Ach.* 88), the notorious starvelings Pauson and Lysistratus, and the homosexual Prepis (*Ach.* 836–59). In this aggressive song of mockery we find united all the groups who are also victims of comic mockery elsewhere. First comes the group of the sycophants, represented by a certain Ctesias. Ctesias is a common name in Athens (Olson 2002:281), and the person meant cannot be identified, but

---

[17] On the role of the *demos* in Aristophanic comedy cf. Reinders 2001.

[18] The term "sykophant" is first attested in Aristophanes' *Daitalês* (fr. 228 K-A), produced in 427. Its etymology has not been explained to general satisfaction ("he who makes figs visible"?) In comedy sykophants are associated with extortion and blackmail, threatening to have their victims put on trial for real or imaginary crimes.

the name is certainly chosen to underline an important characteristic of sycophants, their greed (Ctesias means "the Acquisitive", from the verb *ktáomai* "acquire").[19] Next comes the group of the politicians who held some official position at the time of the production: Prepis (a well-to-do Athenian), Cleonymus, Hyperbolus and Lysistratus.[20] In the case of Cleonymus, who is often satirized by Aristophanes,[21] we can clearly recognize the criteria by which Aristophanes chooses his victim: in the early years of the Peloponnesian War, Cleonymus was politically active – he evidently belonged to the pro-war group surrounding the demagogue Cleon – and seems to have attracted attention by his unusual obesity and gluttony; he is also accused of sexual perversion. On top of these physical and moral defects he apparently belied his name, "he of Glorious Repute", by misdemeanours on campaign that brought the charge of cowardice upon him.[22] Last comes the group of the "intellectuals", beginning with the elderly comic poet Cratinus, who, as a rival of the young, rising Aristophanes, is mocked for trying to make himself look young by getting his hair styled,[23] followed by the painter Pauson, treated as a typical representative of artists, who is pilloried as a starveling, just as Socrates and his pupils are in *Clouds*.[24] In full accordance with the Old Oligarch's analysis, the individuals named are mocked as representatives of groups which can be separated from the common people on the ground of their influence or abilities, and are excluded from the world of the "honest citizen" Dicaeopolis. The exclusion is rhetorically underlined by the repetition of the conjunction *oude* "and not, nor, not even" in expressions like "*Nor* will you be bothered by …". This short choral song can also serve to illuminate the function of comedy in "social hygiene". The latent aggression against the satirized groups is limited to the verbal level; the mockery, the derision, the exclusion, are likewise ritual and symbolic, bound into the festival context of the Great Dionysia, in other words temporary and confined to a specified time of festival licence.

---

[19] Significantly, this choral song is preceded and followed by scenes in which the protagonist Dicaeopolis gets rid of two sycophants without any difficulty (817ff., 910ff.).

[20] Olson 2002: 282–6.

[21] Olson 2002: 100.

[22] Cf. *Peace* 1298ff.

[23] Olson 2002: 284.

[24] Zimmermann 1993: 256–67.

Exclusory mockery in *Acharnians* is especially directed, from the prologue onwards, against "war profiteers".[25] The embassy to the King of Persia, which was on its mission for more than a decade (67),[26] drew two drachmae a day as "separation money" and spent their long mission indulging in oriental luxuries (65–89), comes home empty-handed, but tries to placate the people of Athens with promises which are easily exposed as lies by the protagonist with the eloquent name of Dicaeopolis, "he who is loyal to the city and speaks about its affairs on the basis of justice".[27]

The opposition between the good citizen, who stands up for his homeland in a self-sacrificing way, and the office-holder who gains benefits from war at the expense of the little man, becomes particularly apparent in the confrontation between Dicaeopolis and the general Lamachus. The comic hero strongly emphasises that he has always been a good citizen and an upstanding "Mr. Combatant", not a "Mr. Placehunter", and distinguishes himself and other upright citizens from the group of the war profiteers (595ff.). On the general's indignant question who he thinks he is to presume to speak to him (Lamachus) in that way, Dicaeopolis swings into an all-out attack on office-holders and shirkers. Lamachus, taken by surprise, can only answer, indignant and helpless, "I was elected!" (598). Dicaeopolis represents the average Athenian, who speaks the thoughts of all the citizens who are suffering the effects of military service and of having to abandon the countryside. On the stage, in the illusion of comic performance, he can transform all that in a way that is impossible for an Athenian living in the everyday reality of war. In the assembly, the prevalent disposition is not in favour of a peaceful settlement of the war; but Dicaeopolis can quickly conclude a private peace for himself and his dependants through an intermediary, Amphitheus,[28] endowed with superhuman powers, and betakes himself to the place he has yearned for, his home village, where he can enjoy the pleasures of his private peace all on his own in a thoroughly selfish way. In this liberated

---

[25] Cf. Brockmann 2003.

[26] Euthymenes was eponymous archon in 437/6; cf. Olson 2002: 92.

[27] On the etymology of the name cf. Sommerstein 1980: 180 (on 500): "he who speaks justice on political questions".

[28] On the identification of Amphitheus (a "speaking name" meaning "god on both sides", i.e. both by maternal and paternal descent), cf. Olson 2002: 83f.

space he easily puts right all the wrongs and hardships that daily life in wartime brings. He can refuse with impunity to obey the chiefs of the military, represented by Lamachus; indeed, he can make obscene fun of them and deride the symbols of their power and authority. His voice is failing, he says, through awe and respect of the martial figure of Lamachus and especially of his helmet; so he asks the general to take his helmet off, turn it over and give him a feather from its crest. The unsuspecting Lamachus complies and hands Dicaeopolis the feather, which he sticks into his throat in order to induce vomiting: helmets are now (pardon the expression) something to puke in. The audacity of the passage becomes even clearer if one reads it with its great literary model in mind – Hector's parting from his wife Andromache and his son Astyanax in Homer's *Iliad* (6.466–74).

The triumph of the little man, the honest citizen, over the office-holder, is plainly presented on stage in the latter part of the play. Dicaeopolis refuses to give the general any of the gastronomic delights that he has available in his "free-trade zone" or to take any orders from him (960). There follows his crowning triumph over officials and the powerful (1000). The comic hero is invited by the priest of Dionysus to celebrate the Choes festival, while Lamachus has to march out on campaign; and from these two contrasting expeditions the two heroes make contrasting returns. Lamachus, who in jumping over a ditch has very unheroically sprained his ankle, returns from the field of combat limping and uttering exaggeratedly tragic laments; Dicaeopolis returns half drunk, supported by two attractive girls – and to his humiliation the commander, as he has feared, must endure Dicaeopolis' derision (1174ff.).

The example of Lamachus in *Acharnians* makes it plain why and how Aristophanes subjects a well-known personality to his mockery.[29] The general, like other individuals, becomes a target of mockery and insult in Aristophanes' comedies thanks, in the first place, to the significance of his name. That name, "the Mighty Warrior", by itself makes him the ideal representative of the supporters of war.[30] In the first manifestation of

---

[29] Cf. on this Ercolani 2002, and Ercolani in this volume.

[30] Cf. Ercolani 2002: 228–33 on Theorus, who in *Ach.* 134 is pilloried as the leader of the embassy to Thrace and whose name means "leader of an embassy"; see also above on Ctesias as a representative of the sycophants. Another striking example is Cinesias in *Lysistrata*, a name derived from *kinein* "copulate (with)". cf. Henderson 1991: 151 (§206).

Dicaeopolis' private peace, the festival of the Country Dionysia with its phallic procession and its hymn to the phallus personified as a god, the comic hero joyfully sings that he is now "released from broils and battles and Lamachuses" (270).[31] The pluralization of Lamachus' name makes it very clear that the reference is not just to the individual Lamachus but to all who share his attitudes. In mocking and insulting Lamachus, in coarsely stripping him of his dignity on stage, Aristophanes is placing in the pillory, with Lamachus as their representative, the whole group that he had presented, in the grotesque Assembly scene that began the comedy, as promoting and profiting from the war.[32]

## IV

The insulting of Lamachus in *Acharnians* displays all the characteristics that Sigmund Freud, in his study *Jokes and their Relation to the Unconscious* (1905) ascribes to the tendentious, aggressive joke:

> The prevention of invective or of insulting rejoinders by external circumstances is such a common case that tendentious jokes are especially favoured in order to make aggressiveness or criticism possible against persons in exalted positions who claim to exercise authority. The joke then represents a rebellion against that authority, a liberation from its pressure.                    (Freud 1905/1960: 104f.)

This abuse and degradation of an individual through aggressive jokes is to be seen as a substitute for another kind of aggression:

> Brutal hostility, forbidden by law, has been replaced by verbal invective. … By making our enemy small, inferior, despicable or comic, we achieve in a roundabout way the enjoyment of overcoming him – to which the third person, who has made no efforts, bears witness by his laughter.                    (Freud 1905/1960: 102f.)

---

[31] Olson 2002: 149f.
[32] Ercolani 2002: 225–54.

In comic aggression, in the mockery of prominent citizens, Aristophanes unmasks the arrogance of power of a Lamachus, or of an intellectual like the philosopher Socrates in *Clouds*,[33] or of the tragedian Euripides, whom he pursued with his mockery from 425 (*Acharnians*) onwards.

> Under the heading of "unmasking" we may also include a procedure for making things comic with which we are already acquainted ...the method of degrading the dignity of individuals by directing attention to the frailties which they share with all humanity, but in particular the dependence of their mental functions on bodily needs.
>
>                                              (Freud 1905/1960: 202)

Lamachus' accident makes this very clear: the martial pretensions of the general founder on a mere leap over a ditch, impaled not on an enemy spear but on a stake that happened to be sticking out of the ground there. Similarly, the choral song I have discussed from Aristophanes' *Acharnians* (836–59) shows that the comic poets were particularly fond of using bodily peculiarities and afflictions, and also sexual preferences, as pegs on which to hang their biting mockery. Freud (1905/1960: 201) brings parody into close connection with "unmasking", describing it as a device for degrading and subverting something exalted; and Aristophanes often gives this treatment in his comedies to the exalted pretensions of a Euripides, or to those of the mathematician Meton in *Birds*, who significantly struts on to the scene wearing a pair of tragic *kothornoi* (992ff.), thereby making his arrogant self-importance plainly visible.[34] The foundering of such exalted pretensions on the coarseness and common sense of the protagonist fills the audience with *Schadenfreude*.[35] These unmaskings can (but need not) serve as warnings and admonitions:

> The unmasking is equivalent here to an admonition: such and such a person, who is admired as a demigod, is after all only human like you and me.                              (Freud 1905/1960: 202)

However, authorial intention and audience reception may be two very different things. In *Knights* Aristophanes presents the politician Cleon in the nakedness of his selfish greed for power, and unmasks his pretended

---

[33] Zimmermann 1993: 260–7; Imperio 1998: 43–130.
[34] Zimmermann 1993: 267–70.
[35] Freud 1905/1960: 224; Halliwell 1984: 11f.

concern for the people as aimed purely at serving his own power obsessions; and with this highly political comedy he gained first prize.[36] Yet the same Athenians who had been delighted by this abuse of the most prominent man in the *polis* and had given such a mark of distinction to its author, shortly afterwards re-elected Cleon, whose political "death" they had celebrated in the theatre, as a general, thus confirming his position as one of the most influential men in Athenian politics. In other words, the mockery of Cleon was perceived by the people simply as the degradation of a powerful man, from which no further consequences need flow, and as the exercise of a relief-giving freedom which was tolerated in the context of a Dionysiac festival. Aristophanes himself was afterwards not slow to draw attention to this inconsistency in the attitude of his audience and to rebuke them for it (e.g. *Clouds* 587–94). Aristophanes' criticism of his audience is in harmony with the analysis in Thucydides 3.38 of the way Athenians behaved in the Assembly. Cleon, in whose mouth the historian places this critique of the Athenians, asserts that they do not know the difference between sitting in the Assembly and sitting in the theatre: even when they are in the Assembly, they merely sit back and enjoy the rhetorical *tours de force* of politicians, instead of concerning themselves with the well-being of the *polis*. That comic mockery *could*, however, even at an interval of many years, have a damaging effect, is shown by the case of Socrates. In a retrospective passage in his *Apology* (19b–c), Plato asserts that the Aristophanic caricature of the great philosopher in *Clouds* itself made a significant contribution to the prejudices against Socrates which had become current in Athens and had finally led to his condemnation to death.[37]

# V

The polemical statements of the Old Oligarch have proved to be a true key to the understanding of personal mockery in Old Comedy. The abuse of individuals who stand out in one way or another from the broad masses –

---

[36] Zimmermann 1998: 103–18; Reinders 2001: 168–203.
[37] Cf. Heitsch 2002: 60–62.

whether in wealth, in birth or in intellect – serve primarily to exclude these individuals from the group called "the *demos*" and thereby contribute to strengthen the *demos*' group identity. By this mockery, often coarse and aggressive, the pretensions of these individuals to be "something special" are unmasked as mere presumption; they are thrown down from their high pedestals (literally, in the Meton scene in *Birds*!), are humbled and shown up as inferior to the ordinary Athenian citizen, whether they stumble over their own pretensions, like the mathematician Meton, or whether the aura that surrounds them is brutally dispelled by violence. The function of mockery can be described as primarily one of "social hygiene" within the licence allowed by the Dionysiac festival. The people's aggressiveness – normally dammed up, particularly in times of crisis – against the representatives of the state, against all who have it better than others, all who are extracting (or seem to be extracting) personal advantage from the war, can be diverted down to the verbal level, and through self-identification with the comic hero[38] or with the chorus can be released in fantasies of violence during the performance. This social-hygienic function in no way prevents the poet from drawing attention, through the mockery of particular individuals, to real abuses in society; mockery, and especially mockery of the "unmasking" kind, can have embedded within it the didactical element of admonition.[39] *Knights* shows, however, that the reception of a play by its audience need not necessarily coincide with the didactical intention of the poet. Aristophanes continually extols the educative task of comedy, and in this respect he places comedy on a level with tragedy (*Ach.* 500). Behind or below the jesting and playfulness that comedy has to offer, the poet also aims to perform a serious service.[40] Thus comedy and tragedy are in fact two complementary literary genres in democratic Athens, which by contrasting routes pursued the same objective: the education and enlightenment of the citizenry. For "young children have a teacher who guides them, adults have poets" (*Frogs* 1054f.).[41]

---

[38] Jauss (1982: 264–70) speaks of "admiring identification".

[39] Freud 1905/1960: 202; cf. *Frogs* 686f. This also enables us to explain the measures that were taken against comic freedom of speech (cf. Sommerstein 2002b).

[40] *Frogs* 389f.: "And may I say many funny things and many serious things …"

[41] The author and editors thank Alan H. Sommerstein for translating this paper from the German.

# Names, satire and politics in Aristophanes

## Andrea Ercolani

(Università della Calabria)

In this paper[1] I intend to draw attention to a well known fact concerning Aristophanes' comic technique, namely the employment of "speaking names" in characterising the "comic heroes" of his plays.[2] I believe that a more in-depth analysis of this subject may contribute much to our understanding of fifth-century Attic comedy as a cultural phenomenon. I will first examine a few examples of speaking names, in order to illustrate how Aristophanes operates. Then I will offer a few remarks which I hope will contribute to a better understanding both of Aristophanes' comedy and of its political function.

## 1  Speaking names

By "speaking names" we understand all proper names whose linguistic features evoke, by analogy or contrast, the peculiarities of the character who bears the name. The use of speaking names as a comic device was noted by ancient scholars such as Donatus (*ad* Ter. *Adelph.* 1 = II 12f. Wessner), who remarks that

> *nomina personarum, in comoediis dumtaxat, habere debent rationem et etymologiam ... nisi* (scil. *poeta*) *per* ἀντίφρασιν *ioculariter nomen imponit.*

---

[1] An earlier version of this paper was delivered at a conference on *Form und Funktion der Verspottung in der aristophanischen Komödie* (Freiburg, 4–6 July 2001) and was published in the proceedings (Ercolani 2002). The present version offers various modifications and refinements.

[2] On the idea of the 'comic hero' see Whitman 1964, and also the new interpretation to be offered in a forthcoming work by L. E. Rossi.

The names of characters, at least in comedy, must have a rationale and etymology... unless (the poet) assigns the name jocularly from its opposite.

Aristophanes' speaking names may be classified as follows: (1) partly invented names (2) totally invented names (3) names actually borne by known persons. This final group may be further subdivided into two subcategories: (3a) names borne by known persons, but assigned to invented characters (3b) known persons appearing under their own names.

The case of Bdelykleon and Philokleon in the *Wasps* is paradigmatic of the first group, and – more generally – of the Aristophanic way of playing with names. We are dealing with two fictional names each containing "Kleon", i.e. the main focus of the scenic action and Aristophanes' criticism. The first element of each compound indicates a specific attitude towards the second and common element of the compound, "Kleon", clearly alluding, or better directly referring, to the main figure of Athenian politics of that time. In the comedy, of course, the opposition between Philokleon and Bdelykleon is meant to create a comic contrast on stage to enable the plot to be developed for full comic effect, but it also reflects contemporary political tension: in these very names are mirrored the two main political trends of the Athenian democracy of that time.[3]

If in the case of Philokleon and Bdelykleon Aristophanes only expands the name of the target of the satire; in other cases he invents speaking names from scratch, as for instance Dikaiopolis in the *Acharnians*, Trygaios in the *Peace*, and Peisthetairos in the *Birds*.[4]

Aristophanes also borrows speaking names from contemporary nomenclature. Examples of comic figures whose speaking names were in fact borne by known individuals include, for instance, Rhodippe in the *Lysistrate*, Blepyros in the *Ecclesiazousei*, and Dexinikos in *Wealth*.[5] In some such cases Aristophanes actually intends a reference to an individual

---

[3] On the figure of Cleon in Aristophanic comedy see especially Mastromarco 1993: 341–347, MacDowell 1995: 42–45, Totaro 1999: 180 ff., and recently Mann 2002 with further secondary literature.

[4] For the significance of these speaking names in relation to the dramatic role of the characters see Russo 1994: 34 and Edmunds 1980: 1 n. 1 on Dicaeopolis, Gelzer 1970: 1454 on Trygaios, Marzullo 1970: 181–184 on Peisthetairos.

[5] See Funaioli 1984–1985: 117f. on Rhodippe, Paganelli 1978–1979 on Blepyros, Di Marco 1981 and Bonanno 1984–1985 on Dexinikos.

who bore the name, which brings to the fore the question why that particular figure has been referred to. To be sure, an intention of parody or satire lies in the very reference, but only a more detailed analysis of each instance allows us to understand the workings of Aristophanes' comic technique as well as the complex relations between comedy, satire and politics. I will focus on the case of two speaking names of this kind found in the *Acharnians*, Theoros and Lamachos.

## 2   *Theoros*

Beginning with l. 43, Aristophanes presents the assembly where both Athenian and foreign ambassadors are summoned to report. From l. 134 to the end of the scene the Athenian embassy to the Thracians is dealt with. Theoros is summoned directly to report on the result of his diplomatic mission to the king Sitalkes: "Let Theoros, who comes from the court of Sitalkes, come forward" (*Ach.* 134).[6] The pun in the speaking name "Theoros" has been analysed by Andrisano (1984–5): *theoros* is a *nomen agentis* indicating a duty explicitly analogous to that of our character, i.e. a leader of an embassy.

In order to understand better this scene one should highlight two important aspects: the historicity of the figure of Theoros on one hand, and the historicity of his diplomatic mission to the Thracians on the other.

Let us begin with the latter. An Athenian embassy to the Thracians actually took place a few years before the staging of the *Acharnians*, in the summer of 431 B. C., but the real embassy's leader seems to have been Nymphodoros.[7] The diplomatic mission concluded with the signing of a military alliance with Sitalkes, the king of the Odrysians, who made an expedition against the Macedonian King Perdikkas (429 B.C.), as planned together with the Athenians. From the Athenian perspective the expedition was a ludicrous failure: although 150,000 soldiers were said to have been mobilized, nothing was achieved.[8] It is not surprising therefore that

---

[6] In this paper quotations from Aristophanes' comedies have been given in Alan Sommerstein's translation.

[7] Cf. Thuc. 2. 29. On Nymphodoros see Ziegler 1965.

[8] Soldiers: Thuc. 2. 98. 3 (170,000 according to Diod. 12. 50. 3!). Failure: Thuc. 2.101.

Aristophanes could parody this historical episode four years later, especially if we pay attention to the paradoxical features of the event: the high number of soldiers and the total failure of the enterprise.[9]

The historicity of Theoros' embassy to Sitalkes is, on the other hand, very doubtful. The silence of ancient sources on this point (sources which generally are particularly rich in details: Thuc. 2. 95–101 and Diod. 12. 50 f.) is a strong argument against the historicity of 'the embassy of Theoros'. This indicates that the connection between the representation and the actual event is indeed pure fiction. Theoros' embassy has to be considered as Aristophanes' invention.[10]

Regarding Theoros, at the moment we are not able to make an identification with an individual known outside Aristophanes' plays,[11] but we may confidently assume that he was an Athenian public figure who bore some resemblance to Aristophanes' characterisation. Aristophanes' attacks against him are not only numerous, but also aimed at different aspects of his character. The playwright does not limit his jokes merely to Theoros' speaking name: Theoros is described as κόλαξ in the *Wasps* and as ἐπίορκος in the *Clouds*.[12] The volume and variety of Aristophanes' attacks on Theoros can only be explained by assuming that the target was an historical person, well-known to the playwright's audiences.

We may thus assume the following points: (1) the historicity of the embassy to the Thracians in 431 BC, (2) the historicity of Theoros as an individual, (3) "Theoros" as a speaking name. It follows that the question of the historicity of Theoros' embassy to the Thracians is inappropriate or not meaningful. Rather than at the historicity of the event we should look at the quasi-historical absurdity of Aristophanes' rendering, which makes an historical but second-class figure play an important role in a diplomatic

---

[9] The ridiculous aspect of the history of Sitalkes is confirmed by an analogous parody in Hermipp. fr. 63, 7–8 K.-A. (Φορμοφόροι) = *PCG* V, p. 590, who clearly evokes the same political and historical background by mentioning Sitalkes and Perdikkas.

[10] For a review of the interpretations of 'the embassy of Theoros' see Ercolani 2002: 230.

[11] Against the identification proposed by Bradeen 1964: 48 f., see Sommerstein 1980: 164 *ad* 134 (Theoros).

[12] *Wasps* 42–51, 418 f. and 1236–1238 (with Sommerstein 1983 *ad loc.*); *Clouds* 399ff. ("If he really strikes perjurers, how come, pray, that he hasn't set fire to Simon or Kleonymos or Theoros?"). The joke on Theoros at *Knights* 608 is obscure (Sommerstein 1981 *ad loc.*).

mission of political relevance. It seems to me evident that the embassy scene is played at two different levels: at the historical level and at the fictional one, wherein single elements, far apart in reality, are brought together to form a new story. Both the embassy to the Thracians and the figure of Theoros belong to historical reality, but while in reality the two lines never crossed, in comic fiction they intertwine, resulting in Theoros as ambassador to the Thracians. In short, the embassy of Theoros in the *Acharnians* is the scenic transposition of elements which are in themselves historical but whose resulting outcome is totally absurd and consequently much more powerful from the point of view of the comic effect.

### 3 Lamachos

Let us now turn to the second object of this analysis, Lamachos. Lamachos was a common Greek name, particularly in Athens.[13] However, Aristophanes' target was the well-known general of this name, repeatedly attacked in the *Acharnians*.[14] In this case we should ask ourselves whether Aristophanes chose Lamachos as a laughing stock because he was an historical figure or because he was an historical figure called "Lamachos". At the first glance, this may seem splitting hairs, but on further investigation it may not be. We should consider why Aristophanes in this case attacked Lamachos and not another prominent general, such as Proteas or Perikles, Phormion or Kleopompos, or one of the many others on the list of *strategoi* who would have provided a suitable target.[15]

One factor that may have oriented Aristophanes' decision is clearly the speaking name "Lamachos", behind which the verb μάχομαι and the entire semantic area of "fight" is promptly evoked.[16] It was obvious that this name fitted well with the comic character of the extreme militarist and moreover allowed a whole range of puns by etymology, for example:

---

[13] Fraser *et al.* (1994): 278.

[14] Vv. 270, 566–625, 722, 959 ff., 1071 ff., 1174 ff.

[15] For full listing of Athenian *strategoi* see Fornara 1971, Develin 1987.

[16] On the linguistic features of this proper name, see Taillardat 1992: 161 and Ercolani 2002: 234 n. 1 with further literature; cf. also the analogous name formations with intensive λα- in the *Acharnians*: Λακρατείδης (v. 220) and λακαταπύγων (v. 664).

*Ach.* 270 ff.: ... πραγμάτων τε καὶ <u>μαχῶν</u> // καὶ <u>Λαμάχων</u> ἀπαλλαγείς
"(released) from broils and battles // and Lamachos"

*Ach.* 1071: ἰὼ πόνοι τε <u>καὶ μάχαι καὶ Λάμαχοι</u>.[17]
"o toils and battles and Lamachos!"

Is this explanation enough to justify the massive presence of jokes on Lamachos in the *Acharnians*? In other words, was Lamachos really the only historical speaking name that could have fitted the 'military' play on words and therefore the only possible target of Aristophanes? Were there not further candidates for Aristophanes' jokes?

There is in fact at least one other *strategos* of the period whose name would have had the same, if not a bigger, comic potential, namely Nikostratos. The name "Nikostratos" offered an equally good opportunity as Lamachos as a source for Aristophanes' puns, in view of the fact that the two elements which make up the name both refer to the same militarist semantic sphere: νικάω ("to defeat") and στρατός ("army").

Why then Lamachos and not Nikostratos? My answer is that Lamachos had additional historical characteristics and qualities that strongly influenced Aristophanes' decision. His parody was related not only to a general type of character, that is to say some sort of *miles gloriosus*, but to a particular politician who was probably active inside a specific political group, to which Nikostratos did not belong. Even without taking into account that Lamachos could have been elected as *strategos* before the performance of the *Acharnians*,[18] it may be sufficient to consider the main features of his career to clarify why Aristophanes elected Lamachos over all other figures as the target of his jokes.

Lamachos, probably born after 470 B.C., had already taken part in the 436/5 expedition with Perikles to Pontos; he had probably participated together with Megakles in a diplomatic mission not long before the representation of the *Acharnians* and was *taxiarchos* by the time of the

---

[17] A similar joke in *Peace* 1290–1293: Τρ.– κάκιστ' ἀπόλοιο, παιδάριον, αὐταῖς μάχαις· // οὐδὲν γὰρ ᾄδεις πλὴν πολέμους. τοῦ καί ποτ' εἶ; // ΠΑ.ᵃ ἐγώ; –Τρ. σὺ μέντοι νὴ Δί'· – ΠΑ.ᵃ υἱὸς Λαμάχου. ("TRYGAEUS: Damn and blast you, little boy, you and your battles! You // sing of nothing but wars. Whose son are you, anyway? // – FIRST BOY: Me? – TRYGAEUS: Yes, by Zeus, I mean you. – FIRST BOY: I'm the son of Lamachos").

[18] On this point cf. Ercolani 2002: 237–241, 249–254.

staging of this comedy. A few years later he was one of the Athenian negotiators, who signed the peace with Sparta (421 B.C.). Lamachos, involved in a political career whose end would be the Sicilian expedition as *strategos autokrator*, was in the year 425 B.C., when the *Acharnians* have been staged, surely an important political personality in Athens, and among the most outstanding in the war party. If we add his speaking name to this picture, the rest will be understood.

Both aspects, i. e. Lamachos as an historical personality with peculiar political characteristics on one hand, and "Lamachos" as a speaking name on the other, have contributed to Aristophanes' choice. No case could better fit the saying *nomen est omen*.

A partial confirmation of the importance of the historical role of Lamachos in orienting Aristophanes' choice may be offered by *Thesm.* 801ff.,[19] in which the chorus of women asserts its supremacy over the men and demonstrates this by a comparison of names, pointing out the inferiority of male names like Charminos and Kleophon to female names like Nausimache and Salabakcho (804–5). Two female names, Aristomache and Stratonike, have, we are told, no masculine rival (806–7):

πρὸς Ἀριστομάχην δὲ χρόνου πολλοῦ, πρὸς ἐκείνην τὴν Μαραθῶνι,
καὶ Στρατονίκην ὑμῶν οὐδεὶς οὐδ' ἐγχειρεῖ πολεμίζειν.

And as for Aristomache, "Splendid Battle" – that one at Marathon – and Stratonike, "Army Victory," it's been a long time since any of you has even *tried* to compete with either of them.

The two names Aristomache and Stratonike have been invented *ex novo* by Aristophanes as expressions of feminine military valour.[20] To obtain an immediate comic effect within a complex and allusive joke, in which the vaunted military superiority of women is contrasted with the heavy defeats recently suffered by Athens, Aristophanes has recourse to two speaking names which, on the semantic plane, recall Lamachos and Nikostratos. Thus the possibility existed of coining 'military' names *ad hoc* for the comic occasion. Returning to the analysis of the figure of Lamachos in the *Acharnians*, we may see that, if one attaches importance solely to the latent

---

[19] I am grateful to Alan Sommerstein for having called my attention to this passage.
[20] For these names see Prato 2001: 288 f. *ad loc.*

meaning of the name to explain the joke, one cannot explain why the comedian did not use a more effective invented name, as in the *Thesmophoriazusae* passage, or alternatively why he did not chose the name of a real personage which would be more appropriate for the joke such as Nikostratos (and the positioning of the name Stratonike in *Thesm.* 807 confirms that this would have been the most effective). 'Lamachos' in the *Acharnians* is thus not solely a speaking name associated with a *miles gloriosus*, but a parody and polemical attack against the Lamachos who figured prominently in the political and military life of Athens at the time.

## 4 Satire and politics in the comedy of Aristophanes

The lampooning of Lamachos brings to the fore a fundamental question one should no longer ignore: is the representation of Lamachos merely a cheap laugh or does it constitute a criticism Aristophanes – and ancient comedy in general – addressed against the contemporary socio-political situation? More generally formulated: which function should we attribute to the genre of comedy?

In the course of this paper I have already given some partial answers. I will repeat and clarify some considerations in what follows. Final answers to this question are obviously not at hand, and any reasonable answer should take into account several elements. Despite all this, I am persuaded that an analysis of the *komodoumenoi* and some elements of the communication system show that a political function, in the larger sense, of the comedy was certainly one of the most important. I do not intend to delineate the entire history of the question and will limit my scope to highlighting some considerations that are well known, but often forgotten.[21]

(1) Inside the *polis* everything is political. The theatre is even more political than other literary phenomena, in so far as the stage brought to the fore the same problems that the assembly discussed. I do not suggest that Aristophanes could or intended to stir or influence public opinion (even if

---

[21] For overviews of the discussion see Kraus 1985: 25–30, MacDowell 1995: 5 f. and n. 4, Mann 2002: 105–108. A new approach to the problem is offered by Silk 2000 (esp. 301–349). See also now McGlew 2002.

this could not be absolutely excluded, at least according to Plat. *Apol.* 18c-d and 19c, where Plato highlights Aristophanes' responsibility for the trial against Socrates in 399 B.C.[22]), but it cannot be denied that he contributed through his dramatic representations to debate within the *polis*. I would not go as far as to say that all the elements of Aristophanes' parody and all the subjects of his comedies were directly political, or that they were always perceived as political. Still, we should not forget that the satire of a political figure or even the simple mention of an event, a project or the like, focused the attention of the spectators on that very subject. Let us consider the specific case of the *Acharnians*: by speaking of peace in a time of war, Aristophanes *nolens volens* contributed to the political debate, however we may consider the individual units of the comedy.

(2) A wide range of elements taken from external evidence paint the same picture. The case of the indictment brought by Kleon against Aristophanes as a reaction to the attack of the *Babylonians* is a fact that we can follow up in the *Acharnians*. This clearly proves the political effect of Attic comedy.[23] In this respect one should take into account also the witness of Ps.Xen. *Ath. pol.* 2, 18, who patently attributes a political function to comedy. One should admit honestly that the particular aspects of this political effect elude us. We don't know exactly in which direction and to what degree comedy has influenced politics or the people. Henderson deals nicely with the heart of the question when he states that Attic comedy was basically nothing other than a form of public discussion and political debate: "the theatre was an inclusive forum, open to all".[24] We cannot go much further than that, but to deny this state of things means to misunderstand the meaning of this subject.

---

[22] Cf. Segoloni 1994: 30 ff. (but *contra* Heath 1987: 9–11 and Halliwell 1993: 336).

[23] I will not take into account the various statements regarding the intentions of comedy found in Aristophanes' plays, because of their troubled interpretation (on this point see Ercolani 2002: 245 and n. 56 with literature). As regards the decrees concerning comedy and freedom of speech, which in my opinion strongly support, even confirm, the political interpretation of comedy, see Sommerstein 2002.

[24] Henderson 1993: 317.

(3) In this context the case of Lamachos seems to me particularly instructive.[25] If my reconstruction of Aristophanes' choice concerning Lamachos is right, we have a new piece of evidence that Attic comedy had a political meaning. Other historical personalities were as suitable as Lamachos to be set up as the play's target. But Aristophanes' decision was influenced not only by the foreseeable outcome of a comic effect, but also by the chance to criticize a particular political reality. Aristophanes has brought to the stage neither a *miles gloriosus* nor a sociological satire:[26] he has clearly stigmatised a political position and a political party, a party for which Lamachos was an important representative.

## 5  Conclusions

I will now summarise in brief the results of my investigation:

(1) Real proper names when used as speaking names in comedy were chosen for their comic potential, but the question of speaking names does not end at this level.

(2) One function of speaking names consists in bestowing a given 'historicity' or at least a 'historical' aspect to the scenic events, even more so, when the names were connected to a historical personality (Theoros).

(3) The factors that influenced the playwright's choice in the case of historical personalities, and that produced a comic effect, are of course not always understandable (or at least not completely); in some cases, anyway, the actual political reality of the mocked person is the decisive element. The attack *ad personam* does not seem to be aimed exclusively at producing a mere comic effect: it seems rather to represent the possibility of making a criticism of the person involved in the lampoon, as the case of Lamachos demonstrates, by the use of *onomasti komodein*.
(4) This last consideration leads consequently to the recognition of the political and critical function of comedy.

---

[25] And it is not the only one: one could add *mutatis mutandis* the cases of Kleon, Euripides and Socrates.
[26] See *e. g.* Bruns 1896: 152 ff. (*praesertim* 154), Ehrenberg 1968: 301 ff., Gelzer 1970: 1423, Landfester 1977: 48, Halliwell 1993: 331, Mastromarco 2002: 211 ff.

# Aristophanes, fandom and the classicizing of Greek tragedy

*Ralph M. Rosen*

(University of Pennsylvania)

It is no doubt true that the questions I would like to address in this chapter, which concern Aristophanes' role (and more broadly, the role of Old Comedy) in disseminating and popularizing Greek tragedy, can never be answered adequately, given the nature of the evidence we have to work with. But it is also true that if any progress can be made in answering them, Alan Sommerstein's magisterial editions of Aristophanes, as well as his other voluminous work on Greek drama, deserve a good deal of the credit for it. For during the course of his long-standing scholarly engagement with Aristophanes, Professor Sommerstein has often shown a particular interest in the interaction of comedy and tragedy during the Classical period, and his own contributions to this topic throughout his Aristophanes commentaries have directly inspired the discussion that follows.

In simplest terms, we may put the problem this way: In fifth-century Athens, how was the literary legacy of a tragic dramatist – composing as he normally did with his eye on a single, ephemeral performative event – formed and ensured? In an age of uncertain, probably limited, literacy, when the very notions of "publication" and "readership" seemed inchoate and unstable at best, what were the mechanisms by which tragedians became "classicized" both within their own generation, and in subsequent periods? How did they ensure their own fame? How is it that *some* poets became part of a literary canon, while others were soon forgotten, or at least had a relatively short shelf-life in Athenian culture (which, of course, means, that they rarely make it down to our age)?[1] Another way to ask the

---

[1] I bracket in this discussion the related question of *why* some poets became "classics" in the fifth century, and focus rather on *how*. The two are obviously interconnected, but

question might be this: If there were no Aristophanes, would Euripides (for example) have become the "classic" that he eventually did? What specific role, in other words, did paratragedy play in this process of solidifying a comic poet's reputation? While we cannot expect a simple or monolithic answer to such questions, I would like to suggest in this chapter that the forms of sustained parody and satire directed "against" tragedy in the comic drama of the period can be considered at least one important means by which tragic poets secured a reputation, and in some cases were even turned into classics within their own time.[2] To put it another way, without the consistent "feedback loop", so to speak, that comic paratragedy provided *for* tragedy, the canon of tragic poets, and their individual status within it, might very well have evolved rather differently than it did.

Tragedy is of particular interest in this regard because it was poetry composed, in principle anyway, for the singular and non-repeatable public occasion of a particular festival performance,[3] and so its status as an explicitly "textual" form was especially ambiguous. If the performance itself was really paramount for the poet and audience, one might well wonder what would motivate a poet to produce a version of it in text form after the performance, and who would be its readership. Somehow the lines were written down, of course, but by whom, and when? And to what

---

they take us ultimately in different directions, and the first question ("why?") is probably even more intractable than the second.

  [2] The term "classic" is notoriously difficult to define succinctly; I use the term to refer to a work that has become highly valued by the dominant culture of a given period, a work felt to convey authority as a representative of its genre, and at least an illusion of transcendence. In a trenchant and witty essay, "Why Read the Classics?", Italo Calvino (1986: 125–34) offers one definition (among many) that comes close to the sense in which I use the term in this chapter: "The classics are books that exert a peculiar influence, both when they refuse to be eradicated from the mind, and when they conceal themselves in the folds of memory, camouflaging themselves as the collective or individual unconscious". (p. 127).

  [3] Tragedies could, of course, be revised for re-performance at Athens in the fifth century BCE, or re-performed at rural festivals, and some find the notion of a "single performance" somewhat misleading, (e.g. Csapo and Slater 1995: 2–3). It seems unlikely, however, that a tragedian who composed a play originally for a specific festival would assume at the time of composition that the play would necessarily be re-performed or revived in the distant future. For further discussion, see Pöhlmann 1988: 23–40, and Rosen 1997: 414 n. 4.

end?[4] In order to retain a place in the cultural memory of one's own time, and in that of subsequent generations, one needs a mechanism of iterability, and in the case of drama, if the experience of a performance cannot be reproduced very easily or at all, there needs to be a way – a context and a medium – for the words themselves to be repeated and associated with the poet. A dramatic poet's work, in short, had to assume a life of its own after its initial appearance, whether by becoming a recurrent topic of informal discussion or by circulating in some written medium that made it readily available for reference, such as a papyrus text.[5]

Such "artifactualizing" of an ephemeral performance allows for ongoing critical review and exegesis by supporters and detractors alike, i.e., the groups of people who end up establishing a work's status, for better or worse, within its own time, and often setting its course for posterity. In fifth-century Athens a playwright may well have garnered a certain amount of local stature by simply producing plays with some regularity at the Dionysian festivals, but it would have taken considerably more, I suspect, to turn a poet and his work into something sufficiently reified to invite systematic contemplation and valorization by his contemporaries.

It remains a mystery, of course, what *exactly* took place between the final moment of a play's performance and its circulation for public

---

[4] I addressed this problem a few years ago as it pertained to the second edition of Aristophanes' *Clouds* in Rosen 1997, where I argued that in the parabasis of the extant *Clouds* the poet was wrestling with the notion that he was conceptualizing his "work" – the play itself – as a textual "thing", and that his success with posterity as a "textual" author interested him as much as success in the theaters of Attica. The anxiety that I ascribed to Aristophanes over this may not have been shared by all dramatic poets of the fifth century, but it points up the basic mechanical problems of transmission and reception of a largely performative genre, where "readers" were at best a "secondary" audience. For a review of the limited evidence we have about how early Greek poetry came to be written down, see Herington 1985: 45–48; also Thomas 1992: 123–27, and Ford 2003.

[5] The novelist and critic J. M. Coetzee, in an essay originally published in 1993 (Coetzee 2001: 1–16), entitled "What is a Classic?" (itself alluding to T. S. Eliot's famous lecture of the same title from 1944), suggests that an artistic work becomes classicized when it has survived the "process of day-by-day testing" generation after generation, and "emerges intact". This is an attractive enough formulation for the poetry of fifth-century Athens as well, but highlights all the more acutely the need for a mechanism of repetition. A work obviously cannot be "tested" unless it is readily available for public scrutiny.

consumption, and it is doubtless anachronistic for us to use our own term "publication" for the process by which a play was textualized.[6] Some ancient sources leave us with the impression that tragedies – or probably more accurately, select passages of tragedies – circulated orally, but even a clear tradition oral transmission cannot itself settle whether such material began as texts written down either "official documents" or merely as *aide-mémoires*. One thinks, for example, of Plutarch's famous anecdote in his life of Nicias which recounts how many Athenian prisoners in Sicily at the end of the Sicilian expedition gained freedom by reciting "as much they could remember of Euripides' poetry" (ἐκδιδάξαντες ὅσα τῶν ἐκείνου ποιημάτων ἐμέμνηντο) to their Euripides-crazed captors.[7] Did these luckily literate Athenians memorize Euripides from texts, or had they themselves acquired him from repetitive recitation?[8] It is impossible to say, of course, but it at least made sense in 405 for Aristophanes to depict Dionysus in *Frogs* (52–54) actually "reading" (or at least, reciting from) a written text of Euripides' *Andromeda*.[9] There is little doubt, then, that Athenian culture

---

[6] For an illuminating discussion of this problem, and the various forms of textualizing in the fifth century that might be considered "publication", see Thomas 2003: 170–73: "[We] may at least ask whether a written text was for the author's own record only, for the author to use for revising, for the author to memorize and perform from, or for the author to send out into the wider world and allow to be replicated and sold…"(p. 171). Galen's treatise, *On My Own Books,* offers a richly self-conscious discussion of the many problems of "publication" that beset an author in the face of so many ways of construing "publication". Although Galen was, of course, writing much later (2nd c. CE), the fundamental problems of textual dissemination, authorship and authenticity that he enumerates seem to have changed little since the fifth century BCE.

[7] Plutarch, *Nicias* 29. One wonders exactly how the situation would have arisen in which the Sicilians knew enough Euripides to have conceived a deep "longing" for him (μάλιστα...ἐπόθησαν), yet not quite enough to claim an actual textual familiarity with his work. Numerous scenarios are conceivable (occasional performances of Euripides in Sicily, accounts from foreigners of Euripidean plays that they had seen themselves in Athens, etc.), though none explicitly documented. See Taplin 1983: 89–99.

[8] For a recent discussion of this passage, see Ford 2003: 33. Ford suggests that some of the Athenians – those whom Plutarch describes as "teaching" the Sicilians Euripidean poetry (ἐκδιδάξαντες) – might have relied on a knowledge of Euripides that they had learned in school. I am not entirely convinced, though, for reasons I will address below, that Euripides would have actually become a school text as early as the years preceding the Sicilian expedition. See also Stevens 1956: 90.

[9] See also the frequently cited passage later in the same play, lines 1109–18, in which the chorus claims that the audience can grasp the subtleties of the poetic agon between

was becoming increasingly textual by the end of the fifth century; but less clear is how textual and non-textual forces worked together to construct a poet's reputation in his own time, and secure his reputation for posterity.

Even if we cannot say exactly when dramatic works were fixed in some kind of textual form, we certainly know a number of contexts in which they were disseminated – the many references to symposia or schools as venues for tragic recitation, for example.[10] No doubt such opportunities for verbal repeatability played an important role in maintaining a poet's reputation once it had been established, but I suspect that these venues adopted for their particular purposes poetry that had *already* been classicized, and it was precisely *because* the poetry had been classicized that it was felt to be appropriate entertainment for pedagogical purposes. It is perhaps worth remembering that our own school curricula have not *made* Shakespeare a classic, but rather they adopt him as part of their pedagogical program precisely because he *already is* one.

I would maintain, therefore, that the formative stages in the classicizing of tragic poets must have occurred elsewhere than in dining halls and schoolrooms – but where, and how? In what follows I will attempt to suggest a few places where we might find some insights into these questions, even if complete answers must remain elusive. I begin by positing a simple principle, namely that at Athens the classicizing of a work precedes its circulation as a text for reading; or we might put this more tentatively and say that the existence of a written text need not be a necessary condition for a work to be classicized. I say this to emphasize a point that may seem painfully obvious, but which is often unarticulated, namely, that a work can become a classic without actually being known accurately, or in its entirety. Our own culture may regard Mozart, Shakespeare and the Beatles as classics, but only a very few who hold such an opinion, or would fight for it when it came to establishing canons,

---

Aeschylus and Euripides precisely because "each one has a book" (1114). This passage has been much discussed for obvious reasons; see Dover 1993: 34–35 for a summary of the interpretive problems of the passage and further bibliography. Note also Sommerstein's sobering remarks and sensible analysis of the passage's humor, ad loc. p. 255.

[10] Cf., for example, the conflict between Strepsiades and Pheidippides at the end of Aristophanes' *Clouds* (1362–76) over whether Euripides or Aeschylus was more appropriate as *symposiastic* fare, with discussion below [p. 38ff.]. On schooling as a venue for recitation, see Ford 2003: 24–30.

would be able to sing, hum or recite in their entirety even reasonably accurate versions of their respective works. Similarly in Athens, the proverbial man in the street might have strong opinions about the relative merits of tragic poets, but be able to cite very little, if any, of the actual lines from them. How, then, are their opinions on such matters formed?

I would suggest that the the key players in the classicizing process are what, for lack of a more technical term, I would call "fans", although other synonyms would work just as well: devotees, *cognoscenti*, etc. Before a performative work is fixed and circulated as a text, it will amass a coterie of devotees for whom, for whatever reasons (and there may be many), the works have special resonance. As I noted above, however, for a work to endure, it requires some measure of iterability, even if this means simply some mechanism by which the memory of the event and its author are kept alive. Fans provide this service well in advance of any formal means of mechanical reproduction, for they will take the work seriously enough to continue discussing it among themselves and to proselytize among skeptics about the virtues of their chosen heroes. We catch a glimpse of this process, I think, in the passage at *Clouds* 1362–76, where Strepsiades recounts how he and his son Pheidippides came to blows when the latter repudiated the recitation of Aeschylus, by then an established classic, in favor of the "new" poet, Euripides, whose reputation was evidently still in the process of consolidation. Pheidippides here adopts a kind of critical idiolect so characteristic of obsessive fans:

> ἐγὼ γὰρ Αἰσχύλον νομίζω πρῶτον ἐν ποιηταῖς
> ψόφου πλέων, ἀξύστατον, στόμφακα, κρημνοποιόν. (1366–67)

> Oh yes, I regard Aeschylus as supreme among poets – at being full of noise, incoherent, a bombastic ranter and a creator of mountainous words. [Tr. Sommerstein]

Strepsiades responds that Pheidippides should then instead recite something "from these modern poets, that clever stuff, whatever it is".

> ὅμως δὲ τὸν θυμὸν δακὼν ἔφην· "σὺ δ' ἀλλὰ τούτων
> λέξον τι τῶν νεωτέρων, ἅττ' ἐστὶ τὰ σοφὰ ταῦτα."      1370
> ὁ δ' εὐθὺς ἦκ' Εὐριπίδου ῥῆσίν τιν', ὡς ἐκίνει
> ἀδελφός, ὠλεξίκακε, τὴν ὁμομητρίαν ἀδελφήν.
> κἀγὼ οὐκέτ' ἐξηνεσχόμην, ἀλλ' εὐθέως ἀράττω
> πολλοῖς κακοῖς καἰσχροῖσι. κᾆτ' ἐντεῦθεν, οἷον εἰκός,

ἔπος πρὸς ἔπος ἠρειδόμεσθ'· εἶθ' οὗτος ἐπαναπηδᾷ,          1375
κἄπειτ' ἔφλα με κἀσπόδει κἄπνιγε κἀπέτριβεν.

...But I bit back my rage and said, "All right, you recite something from
these modern poets, that clever stuff, whatever it is." And he immediately
loosed off [reading ἦκ', rather than mss ἦσ'] a speech of Euripides,
about how a brother, heaven forfend, was having it off with his sister by
the same mother. Well, I could take it no longer, and I immediately piled
into him with many hard and foul words; and after that, as you might
expect, we attacked each other insult for insult. Then he jumps up; and
he knocked me and banged me and choked me and pulverized me.

[Tr. Sommerstein]

Even in antiquity it hardly took a professional or an academic to articulate
a theoretical framework for promoting a work of art, when the passion ran
deep enough. Behind this little comic interlude in *Clouds*, then, lies a
parody of Athenian "fandom", the *fanaticism* that was capable of driving
two grown men to fisticuffs in a dispute over literary merit. We may note
how Aristophanes characterizes the extent of Pheidippides' devotion to
Euripides: *Strepsiades*, who recounts the episode, claims not to know
Euripides at all, really: "...whatever it is...", he says  (ἅττ' ἐστὶ τὰ σοφὰ
ταῦτα). People have apparently characterized his work as *sopha*, but
Strepsiades is not even in a position to repudiate this, because (as he
implies) he does not himself have a real sense of what Euripides is all
about. Indeed, Strepsiades seems a little startled by his son's ability to
rattle off a Euripidean speech (ὁ δ' εὐθὺς ἦκ' Εὐριπίδου ῥῆσίν τιν')
especially since he does not seem to have any memory of having seen that
play[11] (the plot seems to come as news to him, or at least he is not familiar

---

[11] In fact, there may even be special significance here in the contrast that Aristophanes
emphasizes between sung verse and spoken or recited verse. Earlier in the passage
(1353ff.), Strepsiades had tried to get his son to sing a classic Simonides tune over dinner.
When Pheidippides objects that symposiastic singing of this sort is antiquated and idiotic,
Strepsiades then suggests that at least he *recite* something from Aeschylus (τῶν Αἰσχύλου
λέξαι τί μοι, 1365). Pheidippides then complies with a Euripidean *rhesis*. It could be that
the contrast here between song and recitation is emblematic also of a contrast between a
classicized work and a work in the process of becoming classicized: to Pheidippides the
modernist Euripides fan, Aeschylus has become old hat, having worked its way long before
into the song repertoire of traditional symposia. By suggesting a *rhesis* of Euripides

enough with it to remember the specific names of the characters: 1371, "...the one where the brother was having it off with the sister..."). I detect in this scene, then, the period in which an author's reputation is being formed and consolidated by his devotees, a group which is able – as Pheidippides is made to do here – to recite speeches from an author who has not yet become canonical and can still be referred to as νεώτερος.[12] Pheidippides, in short, represents a critical player in the process of building a poet's reputation, and establishing the criteria by which posterity would judge that poet's work.

One of the best illustrations from the fifth century of the process by which fans are made comes from an easily overlooked passage in Aristophanes' *Frogs* (771–78). Here the slave Xanthias chats with Pluto's slave in the underworld, who recounts the background to the impending agon between Euripides and Aeschylus:

OI.   ὅτε δὴ κατῆλθ' Εὐριπίδης, ἐπεδείκνυτο
τοῖς λωποδύταις καὶ τοῖσι βαλλαντιοτόμοις
καὶ τοῖσι πατραλοίαισι καὶ τοιχωρύχοις,
ὅπερ ἔστ' ἐν Ἅιδου πλῆθος· οἱ δ' ἀκροώμενοι
τῶν ἀντιλογιῶν καὶ λυγισμῶν καὶ στροφῶν     775
ὑπερεμάνησαν κἀνόμισαν σοφώτατον.
κἄπειτ' ἐπαρθεὶς ἀντελάβετο τοῦ θρόνου,
ἵν' Αἰσχύλος καθῆστο.

---

instead, Strepsiades seems to imply that this form of quotation operates at a less elevated pitch (as if to say, "Okay; if you won't recite a famous classic, then at least give me some non-lyric current stuff you can easily toss off", vel sim.) – one that would not in itself signal a poet's classicized status. Why would Pheidippides have such control of this *rhesis*, and his father no familiarity at all with it? Because Pheidippides, I would say, is made to represent a fan of a poet whose reputation was still in the making in 423 (and which explains why someone like Strepsiades might not know his work – even if he is being disingenuous), and it was his ability to recite from that poet's oeuvre without batting an eye that makes him, and people like him, a key player in the process of classicizing.

[12] Of course, it is difficult to know whether Aristophanes reflects things as they *actually* were, i.e., whether it was credible that people of Strepsiades' generation could claim that they were unfamiliar with Euripides. I suspect it was, in fact, but even if it were not, and Euripides had already achieved a certain classic status by this time (423 for the first production of *Clouds*), what is really of interest for our purposes is the way in which Aristophanes can imagine the unstable and ambiguous status an author might have at the moment when he is in the very process of becoming – but has not yet fully become – classicized. See Dover's (1968) general remarks on this passage, pp. 251–53.

> When Euripides came down here, he began giving display performances
> to the clothes-snatchers and cutpurses and father-beaters and burglars
> who abound in Hades, and when they heard his argumentative speeches
> and his twistings and weavings, they went quite mad over him and
> thought he was the greatest; and then he got so fired up that he laid claim
> to the chair where Aeschylus was sitting.            [Tr. Sommerstein]

This is, in fact, an extremely significant vignette in the play, however
fleetingly it comes and goes, for it offers the key to the play's entire *raison
d'être*: Euripides and Aeschylus must compete with each other, after all,
because Aeschylus' status as a classic is being challenged by a newcomer
whose own fan-base is imagined as threatening to overwhelm and replace
it. Holding the "throne" of tragedy in the underworld, after all, is
tantamount to claiming the status of a classic, and although in practice
there may be nothing to prevent multiple poets from simultaneously being
considered classics, it makes for great comedy if we start with the premise
that only one poet can hold such an honor. As we see in this play,
moreover, this conceit has the added benefit of forcing the poet and
audience to home in with surprising exactitude on precisely what the
*criteria* might be in determining a work's claim to classicism. And it is
through the fan, as this scene makes clear, that we acquire the fullest
insight into these criteria.

The narrative of Pluto's slave bears close analysis in this regard: in the
first place, it is noteworthy that Euripides' plays are made to appeal to
what we would call a "special interest group" of reprobates and criminals.
This is obviously a joke by which the poet projects onto a putative
audience some of the more lurid aspects of Euripidean plots, but even this
absurdity implies that poets rely initially on groups of people who cathect
to their work with a kind of zealotry based on shared critical values. It is
noteworthy, for example, that Euripides' underworld fan-club are said to
respond specifically to a list of technical features, namely his
"argumentative speeches and his twistings and weavings" (οἱ δ᾽
ἀκροώμενοι ‖ τῶν ἀντιλογιῶν καὶ λυγισμῶν καὶ στροφῶν). Of course, a
disreputable crowd such as this would respond to such things because they
would find them useful in pursuing their criminal activities, but the scene
is of particular interest because it highlights the moment when a poet is
imagined to be little known or understood (however delusionally here in

the case of Euripides) except to a small but vociferous group of devotees who can actually articulate a theoretical basis for their affection.

This passage also shows, I suggest, that a fan's devotion to a poet can be extremely powerful even without the assistance of texts, or even the ability to recite from his work. The love of this crowd for Euripides is irrational (ὑπερεμάνησαν), and their affection, while no doubt inflamed by the poet's actual verses, takes on a life of its own that need not rely on an ability to know them in any detail. In fact, the passage seems to imply that this particular audience of reprobates was experiencing Euripides for more or less the first time.[13] They know immediately what they like about the work – plots crafted in a style that reminds them of their own unsavory proclivities, and modes of discourse that can assist them in their criminal ways. This is all raucous parody and gentle social satire, but through it all we catch a glimpse, however distorted for comic purposes, of the role poetic connoisseurship must have played in establishing the reputation of tragic poets.

Another passage in Aristophanes where the process of literary reputation-making is alluded to with rather remarkable self-consciousness is the opening of *Thesmophoriazusae*. Here, as I would like to argue, Aristophanes associates paratragedy in particular with the question of a poet's popularity, as if to suggest (even if the claim was comically inflated) that tragic poets owe a debt of gratitude to comic poets for offering them another venue for the performance of their verses. The play opens with Euripides paying a visit, along with his Inlaw, to the tragic poet Agathon, to ask him if he would impersonate a woman at the Thesmophoria and so defend Euripides and his drama. The women of Athens, as the plot runs, are up in arms about Euripides' allegedly unflattering depictions of them in his plays, and are planning to kill him

---

[13] Euripides is described here as having given "displays" of his poetry to his crowd of adulators in the underworld: ὅτε δὴ κατῆλθ' Εὐριπίδης, ἐπεδείκνυτο (771). The participle οἱ δ' ἀκροώμενοι, ("on hearing…" 774) describes their response, i.e., they went crazy as soon as they heard his sophistically tinged verses, with their twists and turns. We should probably not require Aristophanes to be terribly explicit in a passage like this about when precisely this crowd actually became Euripidean fans, but it is worth noting that he does not describe them as a group who had already been fans when they were alive. The humor of the passage does seem to lie in the conceit that Euripidean poetry was so potentially pernicious that it could convert a gaggle of criminals instantaneously into fervent fans.

for it. Agathon, of course, was routinely depicted as effeminate, and jokes abounded about his sexual relations with men.[14] So the conceit is simply that Agathon would be the logical person to infiltrate the women's assembly and speak in Euripides' defence. The play opens with Euripidean parody put into Euripides' own mouth; the initial dialogue with the Inlaw features an amalgamation of Euripidean lines – some identifiable, others merely inferred[15] – which amount to a comic hodge-podge of sophistic near-nonsense:

EY. οὕτω ταῦτα διεκρίθη τότε.
Αἰθὴρ γὰρ ὅτε τὰ πρῶτα διεχωρίζετο
καὶ ζῷ' ἐν αὑτῷ ξυνετέκνου κινούμενα,
ᾧ μὲν βλέπειν χρὴ πρῶτ' ἐμηχανήσατο
ὀφθαλμὸν ἀντίμιμον ἡλίου τροχῷ,
ἀκοῆς δὲ χοάνην ὦτα διετετρήνατο.
KH. διὰ τὴν χοάνην οὖν μήτ' ἀκούω μήθ' ὁρῶ;
νὴ τὸν Δί' ἥδομαί γε τουτὶ προσμαθών.
οἷόν γέ πού' στιν αἱ σοφαὶ ξυνουσίαι.
EY. πόλλ' ἂν μάθοις τοιαῦτα παρ' ἐμοῦ.
KH.                              πῶς ἂν οὖν
πρὸς τοῖς ἀγαθοῖς τούτοισιν ἐξεύροις ὅπως
ἔτι προσμάθοιμι χωλὸς εἶναι τὼ σκέλει; (13–24)

INLAW: How do you mean, distinct?
EURIPIDES: This is how they were separated originally. When in the beginning the Sky became a separate entity, and took part in begetting living, moving beings within itself, it first devised the eye "in imitation of the solar disc", whereby they should see, and as a funnel for hearing made the perforations of the ears.
INLAW: So because of this funnel I'm not to hear or see? By Zeus, I am delighted to have learnt that! What a wonderful thing it is, I must say, this intellectual conversation!
EURIPIDES: Oh, you could learn a lot more things like that from me.
INLAW: Then is there any chance, to add to these blessings, that you could discover a way for me to learn how to be lame in both legs?
[Tr. Sommerstein]

---

[14] See Sommerstein 1994: 159, ad v. 29.
[15] See Sommerstein 1994: 158–59, and Prato 2001: 142–46.

Two things are noteworthy here: first, the Inlaw is made to be basically clueless about Euripidean poetry – he cannot follow Euripides' line of thought, which is meant to replicate, comically, Euripides' actual verses; clearly the Inlaw is not a fan. Second, though, Euripides claims that he could educate him in all sorts of Euripidean niceties, if (or so he implies, for the subject is immediately dropped) he keeps listening to him repeat his own poetry within a comedy. When the Inlaw expresses his delight in Euripides' "intellectual conversation" (αἱ σοφαὶ ξυνουσίαι, 21), Euripides replies: "Oh, you could learn a lot more things like that from me" (πόλλ' ἂν μάθοις τοιαῦτα παρ' ἐμοῦ.). This seems, at any rate, to be a jocular acknowledgement that his poetry has an active, even propaideutic, afterlife within comic drama.

Agathon too is made to quote his own poetry, or something that must have sounded very much like it, and one gets the distinct impression that we are witnessing the actual formation of a literary reputation as we listen to him. For Agathon, we must remember, had by this time only been performing for about five years (compared to Euripides' multi-decade professional career by 411), and was, to judge from this passage, comparatively unknown. Indeed, one of the reasons Euripides calls on him to begin with, aside from his effeminacy, was because Agathon would be able to operate incognito, whereas everyone would recognize Euripides. The scene beginning at line 29 plays this up in typically comic fashion:

| | | |
|---|---|---|
| EY. | ἐνταῦθ' Ἀγάθων ὁ κλεινὸς οἰκῶν τυγχάνει | |
| | ὁ τραγῳδοποιός. | |
| KH. | ποῖος οὗτος ἀγάθων; | 30 |
| EY. | ἔστιν τις Ἀγάθων– | |
| KH. | –μῶν ὁ μέλας, ὁ καρτερός; | |
| EY. | οὔκ, ἀλλ' ἕτερός τις· οὐχ ἑόρακας πώποτε; | |
| KH. | μῶν ὁ δασυπώγων; | |
| EY. | οὐχ ἑόρακας πώποτε. | |
| KH. | οὗτοι μὰ τὸν Δί' ὥστε κἀμέ γ' εἰδέναι. | |
| EY. | καὶ μὴν βεβίνηκας σύ γ'· ἀλλ' οὐκ οἶσθ' ἴσως. | 35 |
| | ἀλλ' ἐκποδὼν πτήξωμεν, ὡς ἐξέρχεται | |
| | θεράπων τις αὐτοῦ πῦρ ἔχων καὶ μυρρίνας, | |
| | προθυσόμενος, ἔοικε, τῆς ποιήσεως. | |
| ΘΕΡΑΠΩΝ | | |
| | εὔφημος πᾶς ἔστω λαός, | |
| | στόμα συγκλήσας· ἐπιδημεῖ γὰρ | 40 |

θίασος Μουσῶν ἔνδον μελάθρων
τῶν δεσποσύνων μελοποιῶν.
ἐχέτω δὲ πνοὰς νήνεμος αἰθήρ,
κυμά δὲ πόντου μὴ κελαδείτω
γλαυκόν–

EURIPIDES: This is where the famous Agathon has his residence, the tragic poet.
INLAW: What Agathon is that?
EURIPIDES [*declaiming*]: There is one Agathon–
INLAW: You don't mean the bronzed, muscular one?
EURIPIDES: No, a different one; haven't you ever seen him?
INLAW: Not the one with the bushy beard?
EURIPIDES: You *haven't* ever seen him!
INLAW: I certainly haven't – at least not that I know of.
EURIPIDES: And yet you've fucked him–but perhaps you're not aware of the fact! [*The door opens*] Let's crouch down out of the way, because a servant of his is coming out with fire and a myrtle wreath – to make an offering, I suppose, for his master's poetry.
SERVANT: Let all the people close their lips and speak fair; for the holy band of Muses is residing and composing song within my master's halls! Let windless heaven restrain its blasts, let the blue waves of the sea make no noise–                                        [Tr. Sommerstein]

Euripides opens by stating that they have arrived at the house of the "famous" Agathon (Ἀγάθων ὁ κλεινὸς). It is probably true enough that he was, as Sommerstein puts it, the best known of a "younger generation" of poets.[16] We may remember that the setting of Plato's *Symposium* was a party in Agathon's honor after his first victory at the Lenaea in 416. But it is unclear how well his actual work would be known, despite the likelihood that he was developing a following of fans. That is, the processes of repeatability, of contexts in which his poetry could be reproduced verbatim or stylistically replicated were clearly still inchoate. This no doubt explains the joke that follows. After Euripides refers to the "famous" Agathon, his Inlaw again appears clueless: "Which Agathon are you referring to?" (ποῖος οὗτος ἀγάθων;). To this Euripides replies: "There

---

[16] Sommerstein 1994: 159, ad v. 29; Austin and Olson 2004: 61 ad loc.

is a *certain* Agathon…" (ἔστιν τις Ἀγάθων). This may all actually be mere playfulness, and it could well be that no one at the time could *really* be unaware that "the famous Agathon" referred to Agathon the poet. But the joke can really only work if it is at least imaginable that there was a time when Agathon might have plausibly be confused with others of the same name.[17]

There follows a scene in which Agathon's servant appears, and prepares us for the entrance of his master, by offering a pastiche of Agathonian verse, clearly in parody of Agathon's actual verse. The servant here speaks as a fan, both imitating his master's style and explaining it in literary-critical terms:

ΘΕ.  πτηνῶν τε γένη κατακοιμάσθω,
      θηρῶν τ' ἀγρίων πόδες ὑλοδρόμων
      μὴ λυέσθων·–
ΚΗ.           βομβαλοβομβάξ.
ΘΕ.  μέλλει γὰρ ὁ καλλιεπὴς Ἀγάθων
      πρόμος ἡμέτερος–
ΚΗ.                    μῶν βινεῖσθαι;              50
ΘΕ.  τίς ὁ φωνήσας;
ΚΗ.                  νήνεμος αἰθήρ.
ΘΕ.  δρυόχους τιθέναι δράματος ἀρχάς.
      κάμπτει δὲ νέας ἁψῖδας ἐπῶν,
      τὰ δὲ τορνεύει, τὰ δὲ κολλομελεῖ,
      καὶ γνωμοτυπεῖ κἀντονομάζει              55
      καὶ κηροχυτεῖ καὶ γογγύλλει
      καὶ χοανεύει–
ΚΗ.                  καὶ λαικάζει.

SERVANT: Let the tribes of birds be lulled to sleep, let the feet of the beasts that range the woods be bound fast in stillness –
INLAW: Boom didi boom di boom!
SERVANT: For Agathon of the lovely language, our suzerain, is about –

---

[17] One might argue, I suppose, that the scene is funny because Agathon was already so universally famous that only a totally clueless person, such as the Kinsman would wonder who the famous Agathon was; but Euripides' response gives no indication that his Kinsman's reaction was terribly out of line (no quip such as "you complete fool! How could you possibly not know that the famous Agathon must refer to the poet!"). Rather he explains matter-of-factly and patiently that he is referring to an Agathon different from the one the Kinsman mentions.

INLAW [*louder*]:   Not about to be fucked, is he?
SERVANT: Who is it that spoke?
INLAW: Windless heaven.
SERVANT:   – to lay the stocks on which to commence a play. He is bending new verbal timbers into shape, now gluing songs together, now fashioning them on the lathe, and coining ideas and creating metaphors and melting wax and rounding out and casting in a mould –
INLAW:   And sucking cocks.

The language may come across as mannered, and the description of his poetics a little overblown (cf., for example, 53–57), but one can certainly get some real sense of what his poetry must have been like. Euripidean dramaturgy is likewise reenacted self-consciously later on in the same scene, when Euripides reveals his plan to the Inlaw of having Agathon dress up as a woman (88–92). The Inlaw loves his plan, saying (93–4), "An elegant idea, that, and very much in your style! When it comes to scheming, we absolutely take the cake!" (τὸ πρᾶγμα κομψὸν καὶ σφόδρ' ἐκ τοῦ σοῦ τρόπου ‖ τοῦ γὰρ τεχνάζειν ἡμέτερος ὁ πυραμοῦς). Once again, comedy reenacts tragedy and so abets the process by which tragic poets cultivate and maintain their stature.

Since Agathon was a poet whose reputation was still in the process of consolidation, it would make sense that Aristophanes should spend so much time parodying his poetry. Agathon is brought on in the middle of composing a choral song of some sort, and the show-piece is as much Aristophanes' as it is Agathon's. But it is interesting that Aristophanes draws attention to Agathon's unstable notoriety: "Quiet now," he says, "he's getting ready to sing a lyric" (σίγα· μελῳδεῖν αὖ παρασκευάζεται, 99). The Inlaw responds: "What *is* that tune he's warbling his way through? "Anthill Passages" or what?" (μύρμηκος ἀτραπούς, ἢ τί διαμινυρίζεται, 100). It is clear enough that "anthill passages" refers to the twists and turns that characterized Agathon's melodic style, which seemed to share affinities with dithyrambic poetry.[18] But is the Inlaw's cluelessness mere disingenuousness for comic purposes, or does he represent a segment of the Athenian audience who would likewise be

---

[18] Sommerstein 1994: 164, ad loc.; further discussion and bibliography in Prato 2001: 166–68.

relatively unfamiliar with this style? If the latter, the ensuing parody certainly goes far in giving the audience a sense of what Agathon's poetry might have been like, for there follows an extended performance by Agathon in which he assumes the roles of chorus and respondent. The diction is high-flown, and doubtless accompanied by an appropriately outré melodic line.[19] The Inlaw's response once again indicates that he is still in the process of figuring out who Agathon really was and what his poetry was like: "…how delightful that song was! How feminacious, how fully tongued, how frenchkissy!" (ὡς ἡδὺ τὸ μέλος, ὦ πότνιαι Γενετυλλίδες, ‖ καὶ θηλυδριῶδες καὶ κατεγλωττισμένον, 130–1). He then adopts an explicitly Aeschylean mode in asking him further questions about his identity:

> καὶ σ', ὦ νεανίσχ', ἥτις εἶ, κατ' Ἀισχύλον
> ἐκ τῆς Λυκουργείας ἐρέσθαι βούλομαι.                    135
> ποδαπὸς ὁ γύννις; τίς πάτρα; τίς ἡ στολή;
> τίς ἡ τάραξις τοῦ βίου; τί βάρβιτος
> λαλεῖ κροκωτῷ; τί δὲ λύρα κεκρυφάλῳ;
> τί λήκυθος καὶ στρόφιον; ὡς οὐ ξύμφορα.
> τίς δαὶ κατόπτρου καί ξίφους κοινωνία;            140
> σύ τ' αὐτός, ὦ παῖ, πότερον ὡς ἀνὴρ τρέφει;
> καὶ ποῦ πέος; ποῦ χλαῖνα; ποῦ Λακωνικαί;
> ἀλλ' ὡς γυνὴ δῆτ'; εἶτα ποῦ τὰ τιτθία;
> τί φής; τί σιγᾷς; ἀλλὰ δῆτ' ἐκ τοῦ μέλους
> ζητῶ σ', ἐπειδή γ' αὐτὸς οὐ βούλει φράσαι;         145

And now, young sir, I want to ask you in the style of Aeschylus, in words from the Lycurgus plays, what manner of woman you are. "Whence comes this epicene? What is its country, what its garb?" What confusion of lifestyles is this? What has a bass to say to a saffron gown? Or a lyre to a hairnet? What's an oil-flask doing with a breast-band? How incongruous! And what partnership can there be between a mirror and a sword? And what about yourself, young 'un? Have you been reared as a man? Then where's your prick? Where's your cloak? Where are your Laconian shoes? Or as a woman, was it? Then where are your tits? What's your answer? Why aren't you saying anything? Or <u>shall I</u>

---

[19] There is even a stage direction in the R ms. at line 129, *oluluzei*, indicating that his song was to end in a ritual wail. On such "intrusive" stage-directions, see Austin and Olson 2004: 97 ad loc.; also 85 ad v. 99.

find you out by your song, seeing that you don't want to tell me yourself? [Tr. Sommerstein]

Two poetic styles, in other words, interact with each other here. The classicized Aeschylean mode will have been familiar to the audience, and its incongruous application to questions of Agathon's sexual behavior would have surely raised a smile. Agathon's style, however, was less familiar, hardly yet "classicized" (if it ever was, in fact), and it is significant that the Inlaw seeks biographical information from Agathon himself. His question, "shall I find you out by your song" seems to imply that audiences would routinely rely on the parodies of tragedy within comedy for at least some measure of familiarity with tragic poets. Indeed, the main point that Agathon then proceeds to make, that poets must essentially *become* whatever it is they write about, seems to acknowledge just how powerful a force paratragedy might be in establishing (or suppressing) a poet's reputation:[20]

>     αὐτός τε καλὸς ἦν καὶ καλῶς ἠμπίσχετο·       165
>     διὰ τοῦτ' ἄρ' αὐτοῦ καὶ κάλ' ἦν τὰ δράματα.
>     ὅμοια γὰρ ποεῖν ἀνάγκη τῇ φύσει.
> ΚΗ.  ταῦτ' ἄρ' ὁ Φιλοκλέης αἰσχρὸς ὢν αἰσχρῶς ποιεῖ,
>     ὁ δὲ Ξενοκλέης ὢν κακὸς κακῶς ποιεῖ,
>     ὁ δ' αὖ Θέογνις ψυχρὸς ὢν ψυχρῶς ποιεῖ.       170
> ΑΓ.  ἅπασ' ἀνάγκη. ταῦτα γάρ τοι γνοὺς ἐγὼ
>     ἐμαυτὸν ἐθεράπευσα.
> ΚΗ.          πῶς, πρὸς τῶν θεῶν;
> ΕΥ.  παῦσαι βαύζων· καὶ γὰρ ἐγὼ τοιοῦτος ἦ
>     ὢν τηλικοῦτος, ἡνίκ' ἠρχόμην ποιεῖν.

> AGATHON: [*here speaking about the tragedian Phrynichus*] ...he was an attractive man and he also wore attractive clothes, and *that's* why his plays were attractive too. One just can't help creating work that reflects one's own nature.

---

[20] A much discussed passage (146–70), especially line 156, where Aristophanes has Agathon use the term *mimesis* to describe a poet's technique of representing in their work qualities they do not already possess; see Muecke 1982, Stohn 1993, Prato 2001: 182–83, and Austin and Olson 2004: 107–14.

INLAW: Ah, that's why Philocles who's ugly writes ugly plays, and
Xenocles who's a wretch writes wretched ones, and Theognis too, being
a cold character, writes frigid ones.
AGATHON: It's absolutely inevitable, and it's because I recognized that
fact that I gave myself this treatment.
INLAW [*misunderstanding him*]: What treatment was it, in heaven's
name?
EURIPIDES [*to Inlaw*]: Stop yapping now. I was like that too at his age.
When I was just beginning to compose.                    [Tr. Sommerstein]

One has the sense, in fact, that Agathon's concern for how he appears as a
function of his poetry arises specifically because he is relatively
inexperienced. This, at any rate, seems to be the implication of Euripides'
comment to the Inlaw at 173–4, that he "was like that, too, at his age, when
I was just beginning to compose." He means, of course, that he too
attended to his good looks, as Agathon does now, and we can only assume
that he did this for the same reasons as Agathon, namely, because he was
concerned that his poetry would be seen as a reflection of his character
both in its original performance, and in the kind of comic afterlife it had in
venues such as the performance of *Thesmophoriazusae*.

For Euripides now, it is too late to worry about his reputation; everyone
recognizes him and conceptualizes him in a certain way, which is why he
originally sought Agathon's help. Euripides' fame is more or less universal
– he has become an Athenian classic of sorts – but his reputation has been
compromised by what he regards as a gross misunderstanding of his
intentions.[21] And where has he acquired this reputation as a misogynist?

---

[21] Exactly what Euripides' reputation was among the Athenians has always been a
matter of some controversy. He won proportionately fewer victories than Sophocles in his
lifetime, and for one reason or another voluntarily left Athens for Macedonia towards the
end of his life. And then, of course, there is the question of how to assess Aristophanes'
recurrent mockery of Euripides. It strikes me as perfectly possible that a figure who has not
won first prize often could still have been very popular. There's a perennially unstable
relationship at work here between 'official critical notice' (in this case, the judges at
Athenian dramatic festivals) and popular opinion. We might think of the enormous
popularity of certain pop stars in our own era who are continually attacked by 'the critics';
or the reverse– the critics' darlings who never seem to find a large popular following. And
then there are works that are just risqué enough to prevent them from official critical
acclaim, even though people love them. I suspect Euripides might have fallen into a
category such as this. For a sober and thorough examination of the evidence for Euripides'

Perhaps his plays were misunderstood from their first performances on the tragic stage, but it is also the case that *Thesmophoriazusae* itself fosters a parodic version of the serious Euripides, and it is hard to deny that comedy itself remains implicated in his complaints about how he is perceived. No amount of "treatments" of the sort Agathon seeks at this point in his career, in other words, will be able to alter the fixed reputation that he has already acquired from years of producing his own tragedies and watching the comic poets (or at least Aristophanes) create his own variations of them.

I conclude by discussing another easily overlooked passage in *Frogs* which, as I see it, shows Aristophanes having great fun with contemporary notions of classicism and fan-dom. At the beginning of the agon proper between the two tragedians, we find Aeschylus complaining to Dionysus in lines 866–70 as follows:

AI.     ἐβουλόμην μὲν οὐκ ἐρίζειν ἐνθάδε·
        οὐκ ἐξ ἴσου γάρ ἐστιν ἀγὼν νῷν.
ΔΙ.                                          τί δαί;
AI.     ὅτι ἡ ποίησις οὐχὶ συντέθνηκέ μοι,
        τούτῳ δὲ συντέθνηκεν, ὥσθ᾽ ἕξει λέγειν.
        ὅμως δ᾽ ἐπειδή σοι δοκεῖ, δρᾶν ταῦτα χρή. (866–870)

AESCHYLUS: I wasn't wanting to compete here, because we aren't fighting on level terms.
DIONYSUS: Why not, pray?
AESCHYLUS: Because my poetry hasn't died with me, whereas his *has*, so he'll have it here to recite. All the same, if that's what you want, that's what we must do. [Tr. Sommerstein]

---

reputation among his contemporaries, see Stevens 1956, who concludes (94) that Euripides "was chiefly famous as being, after Sophocles, the most distinguished dramatist of his day, unorthodox sometimes and disconcerting, one who roused disapproval in some quarters and was fair game for Aristophanes and his colleagues, but a dramatist whose plays everyone wanted to see…"

The comic inversions and paradoxes here are dizzying: Aeschylus finds it annoyingly ironic that, precisely because he is so well regarded in contemporary Athens, he will not be able to compete on an equal footing with Euripides, because his poetry will remain on earth, and so will not be available to him for ready quotation. Aeschylus is really complaining here about one of the utterly comic side-effects of classicizing: that earthly immortality comes at the expense of immortality in the underworld – or something like that, since the whole scene obviously defies logic! (one might think, for example, that the fact that he already holds the chair of tragedy in Hades would be proof enough that his fame is assured there too – but it is perhaps best not to ask such questions of such a text!). The point is that Aeschylus is made here to contrast his own status as an Athenian "classic" with that of a poet whose reputation is so ephemeral that his verses will die with his body and so (as he implies) leave no lasting impression on earth – no hope, that is, of becoming a classic.

There may also, in fact, be an allusion here to Euripides' famous bookishness, projecting onto him the assumption that he would have *texts* with him from which to recite (*legein*) his plays, while Aeschylus relied on some sort of tradition of recitation from memory; but what interests me here in particular is the way in which comedy itself once again becomes implicated in the process of reputation-making. The paradoxes do not end with Aeschylus' remarks, for there is also the glaring contradiction of the comic playwright, Aristophanes himself, memorializing *through parody* in the here-and-now, performative time of *Frogs* a poet whose verses were said to have perished with him at his own actual death. This passage suggests to me, therefore, that the paratragedy for which Aristophanes was so famous was one of the crucial mechanisms in Athenian culture for maintaining an active forum for public critical debate about the merits of its dramatic poets. As such, it complemented other forms of dissemination and iteration, such as symposiastic or pedagogical recitation, or the occasional re-performance of a play; but it was different from, and more effective in some ways than, those venues. For whereas, as I noted before, these tended to reproduce works that had already achieved some measure of classic status, comedy could interact with tragedy regardless of what its status might have been at a given time. Even if Aristophanes was more interested in Euripides or Aeschylus than he was in, say, Theognis or Xenocles, this interest was not a function, I would argue, of their status as "classics" or "non-classics". He needed to draw on what would resonate with his audiences, and for this purpose, any number of tragic poets – good and bad – were fair game.

Moreover, because comedy is itself a *dramatic* form, produced in the same theater and festival context as tragedy, when it parodies tragedy it serves as a powerful mnemonic for the audience that the original performances of tragedies participated in an agon in which the audience (and more formally, the judges) were invited to compare several poets with each other. Symposiastic recitations may well have been competitive to some degree, but they presented verses wrested from their original context, as showpieces for the display of an individual's skill. Comedy, by contrast, would be able to foster in the minds of its audience a consciousness that the tragedy it parodies was originally competing with other *tragedians*, not simply other recitations, thus assisting the processes by which literary partisanships develop and fans are formed. Thus paratragedy gives the lie to the complaint Aristophanes puts into the mouth of Aeschylus, that the poetry of his rival Euripides cannot survive his death: for the very passage itself, and indeed the entire play, by virtue of its continual engagement with each poet, keeps very much alive the presence of each poet, and ultimately the kind of culture of literary debate in which their own words – whether exact or distorted – are more likely to be preserved. Aristophanes was, in a very real sense, the quintessential fan of tragedy, and paratragedy the means by which he did what all fans seek to do: to ensure that the objects of their devotion always retain their almost talismanic status and never fade from memory.

# Aristophanic spacecraft

## Nick Lowe

(Royal Holloway, University of London)

Notwithstanding some important contributions to our understanding of Old Comic space in the last quarter-century,[1] stagecraft criticism, and the formalist studies of ancient theatrical space that came out of it, have largely passed Old Comedy by. The prevailing orthodoxy on the spatial poetics of Old Comedy is that space and time in Aristophanes are entirely fluid and malleable, and that the relationship between theatrical space and dramatic meaning is therefore much more freewheeling than it is in tragedy's comparatively tight, literalistic set of spatial groundrules.[2] For von Möllendorff, for example, Aristophanic comedy systematically deconstructs spatial categories by drawing a polarising boundary (though not necessarily in *stage* space), and then spending the rest of the play transgressing it. Thus the prologue of the *Clouds* deconstructs inside and out, the *Peace* deconstructs earth versus heaven, and the *Acharnians* deconstructs everything in sight. Von Möllendorff sees this as part of a more general way in which Old Comedy subverts and confounds categoric distinctions, deliberately muddling up things that ought to be kept apart.

I want to argue that the assumptions underpinning this consensus need revisiting. In what follows, I aim to show that the mapping of space in Aristophanic comedy is not anarchic or incoherent; that our impression of boundless lability arises from a misunderstanding of a small number of distinctive but coherent genre conventions; and that space is as important a

---

[1] As well as the older contributions by Dover 1966, Dale 1957, Russo 1961, and Dearden 1976, important recent contributions have been made by Thiercy 1986, Issacharoff 1987, Handley 1993, Pöhlmann 1995, von Möllendorff 1995, Poe 1999, 2000, Wiles 2000, 2003, and in Cusset *et al.* (2000). Sommerstein 2002a is an essential resource, not least as a directory of often fundamental discussions in his commentaries on the individual plays.

[2] I fell for this one myself in Lowe 1988, to which the present paper is a palinode.

shaper of narrative and theme in Aristophanes as it is in tragedy, and for the most part in ways that are far more similar than they are different.[3] I propose to build up a model of how theatrical space functions in Aristophanes by offering a few observations about the construction and thematic significance of theatrical space in each extant play, taken not chronologically but in ascending order of complexity and difficulty. At the end of the tour, I shall try to draw the threads of the survey together and suggest some general conclusions about the principal differences between tragedy and comedy in terms of the relationships they construct between space and meaning.

I begin with the play that seems most tragedy-like in the relationship it constructs between space, action, and theme. *Wasps* is the play usually felt to come closest to observing a tragedy-like "unity of place". Indeed, I shall argue that it is the *only* play of the eleven in which the *skene* and its door continue to represent the same building with the same owner from the opening lines of the play to the end.[4] More significantly, however, it is a play built entirely around a familiar spatial dynamic from tragedy: a series of blocked, delayed, or thwarted exits, which repeatedly frustrate the attempts by a central character to leave the stage by an *eisodos*. This configuration of space and action around a goal of escape is a pervasive pattern in tragic and satyric plotting, activated in different ways by *Medea*,

---

[3] Although in what follows I try to make no assumptions on the major controversies of Aristophanic staging, it will be apparent that my instinctive position is closest to that of Thiercy (1986, 2000). In particular, I incline to side with the "London school" of Dale, Webster, and Dearden in favouring a single *skene* door (the position Handley terms "monist", against such "pluralists" as Dover, Russo, and Pöhlmann), without however sharing their belief in widespread and casual use of the *ekkyklema*. Two early plays, *Clouds* and *Peace*, are difficult to stage with one door; *Acharnians*, *Thesmophoriazusae*, *Frogs*, and *Ecclesiazusae* may use one door or two; the remaining five plays clearly assume one. No fifth-century tragedy uses more than one door, and I find it easier to try to argue *Clouds* and *Peace* down to one door than to believe that such a potent theatrical resource (as New Comedy demonstrates) was so pitifully thinly used. The debate mostly comes down to what we read at *Clouds* 125 and what we make of ἔξελθε at 1486; I have no new solution to either of these.

[4] This unusually early specificity of identity for the *skene* would be connected to the unique role of the *skene* in the opening visual puzzle, if only we could feel confident that the net over the building was somehow visibly as well as verbally indicated.

both *Electras*, *Philoctetes*, *IT* and *Helen*, *Orestes*, *Cyclops*, and the end of *OT*. Here, the blocking of Philocleon's exit from the stage gives spatial form and tension to the play's central idea: the attempt to confine Philocleon's energies to the private sphere of the household, instead of unleashing them on the civic world of the *polis*.

This spatial tension neatly propels the play's actions, themes, and eventual twists. At first Philocleon is unable even to get out of the house on to the stage, because he is literally a prisoner in his own *oikos*: the *skene* has a net over it, guards posted at the door and on the roof, all openings sealed. After a series of failed escape attempts in the prologue, he eventually manages to emerge in the parodos with the help of the chorus of fellow jurors. But the agon is then devoted to trying to persuade him not to complete his intended journey by leaving the stage and going off to court; and Bdelycleon's triumph is immediately followed by the domestication of the civic apparatus of justice in the trial of the dogs, where all the personnel of the trial are summoned from inside the *oikos*, and the trial itself is played out in the front yard. Bdelycleon's victory is sealed when Philocleon, apparently now fully domesticated, is persuaded to re-enter the *skene* rather than leaving by an *eisodos*. The final stage of his reform will be to return him to the community, but now in a private rather than a public role, by allowing him to attend a symposium instead of a court. Thus when Philocleon finally gets to make his long-delayed *eisodos* exit at 1292, it is on terms very different from those of his original attempt. But the scheme backfires; the old dog learns his new tricks rather imperfectly, and the energy that hitherto has been contained by channelling it into democratic mechanisms of power is now an anarchic individualistic violence unleashed on the *polis* and unchecked by civic controls. He returns to the stage at 1326 on his own terms, trailing devastation; Bdelycleon manhandles him into the house with some difficulty at 1449, in the middle of a sentence, but even this last attempt at containment is short-lived; the old man causes pandemonium inside, and breaks out one final time to demonstrate his triumph with a frenetic physical finale, which concludes with hero and chorus leaving the stage and escaping into the outside world in Aristophanes' most show-stopping exodos.

As always, there are a number of incidental questions one could tackle about details of staging, such as whether one *eisodos* was consistently used for the court and the other for the symposium, but these do not affect the clarity or thematic pointedness of the play's overall spatial dynamics. The important question is, do the other plays exhibit similarly purposeful spatial patterning? I want to suggest that they do – but not always in ways so recognisably congruent with tragic stagecraft.

At the opposite end of Aristophanes' career, *Plutus* is another play generally credited with a tragedy-like unity and literalism of location, set entirely outside the door of Chremylus' house. Its action uses spatial patterns of theoxeny and cult introduction to negotiate a strongly-thematised relationship between private and public spaces in which the door to the hero's house is the principal boundary, and movements across this boundary mark key phases in the establishment and extension of the new utopian order. The prologue begins with a tragedy-like *nostos* from abroad, the arrival of Chremylus and Cario costumed in a clutch of Delphic signifiers as they follow the blind god on to the stage, and at the end of the prologue Chremylus persuades Wealth to enter his household, as represented by the *skene* door. Chremylus now enjoys the benefits of the god's enrichment all on his own, and friends come trooping to his door to find out about the house's secret. But it is made clear from the start that this is just a temporary phase during the preparations for an expedition to the shrine of Asclepius. Departure for the sanctuary is temporarily blocked by the arrival of Poverty, but she withdraws from the stage after the unresolved agon, and the god is escorted from the house and off by the parodos. When he returns, he has his sight back, but remains under Chremylus' control: he re-enters the house and turns it into a kind of indoor utopia, and the door now becomes the focus of a series of encounters between his gatekeepers Chremylus and Cario on the one hand and the wider human and divine world on the other, as a succession of newcomers try to gain access to this private utopia and are judged, being either admitted or turned away. The play closes with Wealth finally transferred from this individualistic private space to the public space of the Acropolis, his blessings released at last from one man's household to the *polis* as a whole.

Though a different kind of spatial plotting from *Wasps*, this uses many of the same spatial shorthands, particularly in the use of the *skene* door as a thematically charged boundary between private and public spaces, and of *eisodoi* as a route into the wider world outside.[5] But there is one important difference from *Wasps*: this time the location is not established, nor any identity for the *skene* even hinted at, until 228–31. The initial visual teaser, two sighted men following a blind tramp, presumes that the blind character is wandering around aimlessly and without destination; it is only at the very end of the prologue that the door is given an identity.

This illustrates a fundamental rule: even in comedies which otherwise observe a strict unity and specificity of location, prologues can be, and usually are, essentially *atopic*. Comic prologues have a good deal of work to do; one of the reasons they are so much longer than tragic prologues, typically around three or four times the length, is that they have to construct an entire universe *ex nihilo*. There are no shortcuts; as Antiphanes' famous syncrisis ruefully notes, in comedy it is not possible simply to say "This is Thebes and the king is Oedipus", and have the audience instantly know what the *skene* represents and who all the characters are. Instead, in an Aristophanic prologue the place, time, and situation of the play are progressively constructed out of a Brookian empty space. The world of the play is only gradually demarcated from the world of the audience, with a repertoire of standard devices used to phase it in: warm-up routines for one or two performers, joking directly with the audience; visual puzzles in the opening tableau which challenge the audience to decode the situation before the dialogue lets them in on the secret; teasers in the dialogue that hint at the subject of the play, but then postpone any further revelation. Above all, however, the prologue is a place where space is still in the process of being created. What tends to fix location is the arrival of the chorus – and with them the stability, continuity and in most cases the very title of the play.

Let us turn to a slightly more complex case again. *Knights* is another play generally thought of as obeying "unity" of setting, and this time, unusually, the prologue actually identifies the *skene* and its door in the opening lines. This is the house of Demos: the space that has been infiltrated, taken over, and perverted, its citizen householder displaced by a foreign chattel of his own purchasing. As in *Plutus*, there is a strong

---

[5] The usual assumption is that the *eisodoi* were used consistently according to the tragic model of one into-town, one out-of-town: a plausible but not obligatory construction.

identification between the house and the householder, which here extends to the body: in more ways than one, the slaves are competing as *erastai* for the penetration of Demos' entrance. The first half of the play is built around the competition for the right to enter the *skene*, which is played out mostly in front of the door but decamps offstage during the parabasis to the Paphlagonian's other home ground of the Boule. On their return to the house following the Sausage-Seller's victory in the Boule, neither enters the building; instead, in the play's long-postponed climactic entry Demos himself comes out, and is the object and judge of an onstage competition for his favours. At the end of the contest, Demos selects the Sausage-Seller rather than the Paphlagonian to accompany him back into the house, leaving the Paphlagonian stranded and displaced; and when they leave the house again for the exodos, the party of Demos and his new servant Agoracritus heads for the prytaneum, while the text ends with the Paphlagonian not merely excluded from the house but expelled as a *pharmakos* from the entire city, to be an example to οἱ ξένοι.

We may, however, note three complications. First, even while the *skene* continues to represent the house of Demos, at 749–51 the agon adjourns to the Pnyx. It is clear from 751's ἐς τὸ πρόσθε that at this point the action moves from the door to the orchestra, shifting the scene on the axis between periphery and centre that Wiles (1997) has identified as a major constructor of oppositional categories in tragedy. Dale's influential term for this was "refocussing": a change of scene evoked by a subtle reidentification of the setting in dialogue and action rather than by any visible alteration of background. The most famous example, which seems to operate in a very similar way to the *Knights* scene, is in *Choephori*, where the action moves from the tomb of Agamemnon in the centre of the orchestra to the palace represented by the *skene*. We are not to imagine that Clytemnestra has simply buried Agamemnon in her front garden; these are discrete locations in the same set, are invoked in separate and successive scenes. The more literalistic tragedy of the post-Aeschylean era avoids this device; but as we will see, it survives in comedy at least as late as *Thesmophoriazusae* and the prologue of *Frogs*.

A second curiosity: after the agon there is an extended routine of fetching and carrying where the Paphlagonian and the Sausage-Seller compete to produce first oracles and then luxury items from within the *skene*. What does the *skene* represent during this scene? If it is still the house of Demos, the whole spatial dynamic of the play seems to dissolve if the Sausage-Seller is now granted the prize of entry to the house. One could argue that such an entry is not entirely inappropriate, given that the Sausage-Seller is gradually encroaching anyway and this is not a permanent or invited entry. But, to be literal-minded for a moment, what are the Sausage-Seller's oracles doing in Demos's house, which he has never entered in his life? Is Agoracritus bluffing, and improvising oracles on the spot while pretending to read from any old shopping list found in the house; or is he using a second, different *skene* door, something that has no obvious support in the text? There is a simpler, long-recognised solution: as tends to happen in scenes of comically-elaborate fetching and carrying, the *skene* is momentarily reverting to an anonymous prop-store "inside", even when, as here, it goes against the grain of the play's overall spatial thematics.

We shall return to this later; but before we leave *Knights*, a note is needed on the old debate about the identity of the door in the final scene following Demos' rejuvenation. At 1323 and 1327 Demos is described as now residing "ἐν ταῖς ἀρχαίαισιν Ἀθήναις", and at 1326 the doors of the *skene* creaking open are described as the Propylaea. For most commentators, this is enough to identify the *skene* as now representing the Acropolis. This is not a necessary inference; all three references can be taken as comic metaphor. But it is of course a metaphor which fits unusually well with the allegorical basis of the play, which rides on a mapping between the private space of the *oikos* and the body and the public space of the democratic *polis* – a mapping enabled, like the personification of Demos himself, by the demagogic catchphrase δοῦλοι δήμου, "slaves of the people", which the play has ingeniously reified in creating the world's earliest extant allegorical drama.

There are a clear parallels here with the spatial dynamics of Aristophanes' other penetrating comedy of politics and the body, *Lysistrata*. The spatial logic of the door here has long been recognised: the whole play is built around the women's refusal to the men of penetrative access to their interior spaces until the treaty is agreed, whereupon the gates are open and the menfolk of Hellas are free to come in and party. For present purposes we need only note two things about the very insistent role of the *skene* door as the main constructor of action and meaning in this play. First, this is another play in which the location is established only at the end of an atopic prologue, which seems to have gone to some pains to avoid using any doors whatever.[6] Second, though the door for once has a fairly stable identity throughout the play as the Propylaea, the oppositions it constructs are much more polysemic than that. Some are the standard "Female Intruder" oppositions familiar from tragedy: inside/outside, private/public, female/male. But others are constructed by the fusion of public and private space deriving from (i) the assimilation of a public gateway to a private doorway, and (ii) the eroticisation of the gendered interior space with the female body. Thus the door comes also to construct oppositions between sacred/secular, penetrated/penetrating, consummation /frustration, and more, and a potentially limiting construction of spatial boundaries becomes an unusually rich engine of action and meaning.

An instructive contrast can be drawn here with *Ecclesiazusae*, which like *Wasps* and *Knights* does identify the *skene* door in the opening lines.[7] Despite the similarity of scenario with *Lysistrata*, the spatiality of this play offers quite different thematics. There is no attempt by the outside world to penetrate the *skene* door; quite the reverse. The conspiracy is hatched in a domestic space, exported to and sanctioned by the citizen body in the offstage civic space of the assembly – mirroring the way the revolution itself is founded on an export of domestic economy to the level of the *polis*. The many uncertainties surrounding the use of doors in this play, and particularly over which entries are from a *skene* door and which are from an *eisodos*, do not affect the general spatial dynamic of the play, which centres on a communalisation of all civic space played out in a transfer of goods from the private space onstage and indoors to the public space offstage via the *eisodoi* – whether those goods be the parade of kitchen equipment Chremes escorts from his onstage or offstage house to pool with the common store, or the rights of sexual access represented by

---

[6] Others may be more easily persuaded than I that the ἐξέρχεται in line 5 means that Calonice is coming out of a skene door which is never acknowledged again in the rest of the prologue.

[7] I elide discussion here of the old problem as to whether this is a two- or three-door play or a one-door-two-windows play; but note that the text offers no confirmation that the house of Praxagora and Blepyrus is on stage.

the female-controlled door or doors in the hags scene. There seems at least
one reidentification of the *skene* front, unless we posit a three-door *skene*
and allocate multiple owners to each door; but the key point, on either
interpretation, is that the location remains a domestic street-scene
throughout, and the communist utopia is spatialised offstage via the
*eisodoi*. The most useful comparison is not with *Lysistrata* but with the
spatial construction of the process of utopianisation in *Plutus* – though
there the utopia is contained *within* the domestic space until the final
minutes of the play.

    *Clouds* is likewise quite a difficult play to untangle in points of detail,
and it may be that the revision of the text has confused the issue; in
particular, there is a notorious problem over the number of doors, which
can be resolved in a number of ways, none of them very satisfactory. But
here again a few uncontroversial things can be said about the overall
spatial logic that are not affected by the problems highlighted by Dover.
First, Strepsiades' house, if shown on stage at all, is never a *significant*
space; there is, for example, no opposition constructed between the doors
of the kind we find routinely in New Comedy, which may incline us to
prefer a single-door staging with perhaps a brief change of ownership.[8]
Instead, the action and themes are organised entirely and essentially
around the door to the Brain Shop, which signifies the point of entrance to
Socrates' school on a number of levels that go beyond the literal. From the
very first mention of the school in line 92ff. ("Do you see that door and
that little building? ... It is in there that the men live..."), the school is a
school in three senses of the English word: it is a *building* with a door, but
it is also a closed *sect* with its own strict rules of admission and exclusion,
and it is a body of *teachings* into which one has to be formally initiated.

    Crucial to this concept is that we never see inside the school. Despite
the brief scene at 184ff. where the door apparently is opened and some of
the students are exposed to Strepsiades' view (perhaps, but perhaps not, on
the *ekkyklema*), the interior of the school remains a world apart.
Strepsiades spends a good deal of time and comic energy trying to get in,
and is almost immediately thrown out; Phidippides then is sent in in his

---

[8] This is Thiercy's preference, but he has not entirely disposed of Dover's original
counter-arguments, which remain troubling to the monist position.

place, and upon graduation is returned to the community. But it quickly transpires that anything that emerges from Socrates' door is a potential threat to the good order of the *polis*, and that anyone who attempts to take Socrates' teaching out of the school into the wider world is letting some dangerous genies out of their bottles, necessitating an extraordinary and unparalleled finale in which the *skene* itself is set on fire.

*Thesmophoriazusae* is normally thought of as a play with a single scene-change, from Agathon's house where the prologue is set to the Thesmophorion where the rest of the play is confined. Closer examination shows that, once again, the space of the prologue takes time to come into focus: there is an initial visual teaser where Euripides is dragging the In-Law around the stage, the door is singled out as a destination, and finally the ownership of the door is announced, before Agathon appears in person on an *ekkyklema* that not only confirms the ownership but establishes the door as a genred space, a point of interface to the world of tragedy. Once Agathon closes his door, however, the sense of location dissolves, and once again a fixed setting is constructed only with the arrival of the chorus. The festival setting constructs a world of gender inversion marked off in space and time from the normal world, and an initial Telephean plot of infiltration modulates into a satyric-Euripidean plot of captivity as the In-Law's disguise is exposed. The challenge is then to extricate the hero from this world turned upside down, by deliberate quotation of the spacecraft of Euripidean rescue plays. It becomes, like *Wasps*, a play of thwarted exits; but this time, the space of captivity is not the *skene* interior, which plays no part after the prologue and reverts instead to an anonymous prop-store,[9] but, uniquely, the entire orchestra.

The ambitious spatial structure of *Birds* seems at first quite closely parallel to *Plutus*. We begin with two humans following a non-human guide (in this case a pair of prop birds) to a destination signalled in the opening dialogue as the door to a house, here the abode of Tereus the Hoopoe. After some initial hesitation over recognising the door for what it is, Pisthetaerus and Euelpides then spend the first half of the play negotiating entry to the world it signifies. But this activates a quite different set of oppositions to the broadly tragic polarisation of domestic/

---

[9] See especially Austin & Olson 2004: xxii.

civic in the plays we have been considering so far. Though there is a token attempt to anthropomorphise the Hoopoe's space as the abode of his family, the door and the negotiations around it develop the Hoopoe's significance as a liminal, mediating figure between the human and avian worlds. At last the agon concludes with the two mortals entering the door, and re-emerging after the parabasis transformed into honorary members of the avian realm. Hereafter, however, the Hoopoe drops from sight, and the door becomes Pisthetaerus' personal base and centre of operations. The abortive sacrifice scene moves out from the doorway into the orchestra, but is forced to withdraw indoors again as the doorway becomes a prop-store interior under Pisthetaerus' individual command, from which he dispenses ornithomorphism to selected deserving comers. Unlike in *Plutus*, there is no question this time of letting anyone else inside; and his final triumph is sealed with a wedding procession whose destination is unclear in the text and has sometimes been thought to involve an unusual exodos into the *skene* door.

Like *Plutus* and *Knights*, this is a systolic play of two halves on the *Agamemnon* model, with an inwards movement followed by an opening-out and disgorgement. Though there is no suggestion of a scene change, the ownership and significance of the *skene* door are both transformed the moment Pisthetaerus replaces the Hoopoe as its gatekeeper. The first half is a tight, coherent door play, with the two refugees from an offstage world well lost struggling to gain admission to the door and the world it signifies in the face of opposition from inhabitants inside and out. The second half, in complete contrast, displaces the axis of action from the horizontal plane to the vertical, using the performance space as a mediating zone between a uniquely complex array of offstage spaces. Having constructed its central conceit of the mid-air *polis* as a buffer zone between earth and heaven, the play then seeks ways to verticalise the horizontal space of the *skene* and orchestra to express the trade war between earth and heaven: so with the *mechane* for Iris's entry, and Prometheus' parasol to hide from the overseeing eye of Zeus. But much of this opposition of offstage spaces in the vertical axis has in practice to be horizontalised between the two rather overworked *eisodoi*, which need to give access to Athens on the one hand and Nephelococcygia and Olympus on the other. The sequence of entrances and exits in the text suggests that a consistent opposition between one terrestrial and one supernal parodos may not in fact have been followed, and on any account the staging of the final wedding procession seems rather inelegant. Nevertheless, it is striking that unity of location seems to have been preserved throughout in defiance of what would seem a temptation to move the scene to Nephelococcygia in the second half.

Despite these remarkable spatial arabesques and changes in door ownership, the actual stage setting of *Birds* is still closer to *Wasps* in its essential unity. When we think of Aristophanic comedy as spatially freewheeling and fluid, we are usually thinking primarily of a play such as *Frogs*. This, after all, is the play where the action begins with an arrival at a door signifying the house of Heracles, departs on a journey through the underworld in the course of which a whole series of landmarks are conjured and discarded in rapid succession, and fetches up at a door representing the palace of Pluto. Yet I would argue strongly that the spatial logic remains surprisingly clear-cut and focussed throughout. For one thing, it needs stressing that the shifts of setting are confined to the prologue; thereafter, the play observes strict and specific unity of location. From line 440 to the end, the *skene* represents Pluto's palace, and its interior harbours an assortment of infernal denizens, whether sinister, benign, or poetical. As in other plays, the arrival of the main chorus in the parodos coincides with a fixing of a previously fluid or anonymous location. Secondly, that location itself has been strongly signalled from the outset as the destination of the journey; and not only that, but each of the landmarks en route was specifically mentioned, in order, by Heracles in his original instructions for the journey. So although this is the most spatially fluid of Aristophanes' prologues, that fluidity is anything but chaotic: there is a strong sense of sequence and destination, apparently drawing on the kind of katabasis routefinder instructions we find in the "Orphic" gold leaves. And finally, once the *skene* acquires its stable identity, it becomes the framework for a consistent and sustained set of categoric oppositions. Dionysus' goal is to take a poet out of the palace and offstage into the world; and the contest ends with the victorious Aeschylus returning with Dionysus to the land of the living, in an exodos which once again carries the fruit of the comic resolution out into the world, completing the initial kathodos with an anodos into the world of the city and the audience[10] while the defeated Euripides returns through the *skene* door to the palace of the dead.[11]

By this stage, we are in a position to make sense of what might seem the least spatially coherent of all the extant plays. *Acharnians* is certainly the play that jumps around most: beginning with a prologue on the Pnyx, moving to Dicaeopolis' house (perhaps in his home deme of Cholleidae), making an abrupt detour to Euripides' house (on Salamis, according to one tradition!), then back to Dicaeopolis for the rest of the play, but culminating in a prop-laden routine between Dicaeopolis and Lamachus where the *skene* simultaneously represents both their houses at once.

Most of this falls nevertheless into patterns which I hope by now are reasonably clear. It should not surprise us, for example, that the *skene* only gets identified as a particular house in the closing lines of the prologue; nor that the rest of the prologue has had a quite different setting, in which the *skene* door seems to play no part. What we seem to have here is another case of refocussing along the axis between orchestra and door, with the public space of the Pnyx dissolved as the assembly breaks up. It may not be coincidental that the only instance of refocussing on this axis in a later play at a point subsequent to the arrival of the main chorus is again a Pnyx scene, the agon in *Knights*. This mirrors the movement of the play from the public sphere to the private, as Dicaeopolis takes upon himself the responsibility and rewards of peace abrogated by the city in the assembly.

From this point on, the play is about Dicaeopolis' privatisation of public space. The first thing he does after the parabasis is to mark out the boundaries of his market on the stage, and the goods he trades with the Megarian and Boeotian are traded in and out of his doorway. Then comes the sequence where first the farmer and then the wedding party come to Dicaeopolis' door to cadge a few drops of peace, and he takes relish in

---

[10] The text leaves it unclear whether Dionysus as well as Aeschylus appeared in the final scene, but as Sommerstein notes (ad 1500) it would be astonishing if the god's repeated promises to lead the poet back were left unfulfilled. The protagonist may have taken Pluto for this scene, leaving Dionysus to a mute.

[11] Euripides' exit is not marked, but he surely enters the *skene*, either at 1481 or directly after 1478 (so Sommerstein ad loc.); certainly not "at a run, tearing his hair and wailing" (Dover ad 1481).

deciding who to favour and who to turn away; and the play closes with an elaborately symmetrical routine where Dicaeopolis and Lamachus are called out of their house or houses to answer very different invitations to serve their city, and both limp home incapacitated at the end having given their all in very different ways. This final sequence reintegrates the public and private spaces by an exodos which, as usual, exports the final situation of the play out of the play and into the world of the audience and the performance.

The misfit in this otherwise-clearcut scheme is the Euripides scene. Even in context, it is a complete bolt from the blue; Dicaeopolis begins his chopping-block speech, then suddenly walks out of the middle of the scene at 394 to go and visit Euripides, before returning in Telephus costume to complete the scene. What makes this possible at all is the fact that the scene has refocussed downstage into the orchestra for the block scene, so that the *skene* door can now become as it were another point on the circumference. There is a parallel of sorts in the way the *Knights* suspends the identity of the *skene* for the oracle scene, and then restores it for the subsequent entries of Demos and Agoracritus. Nevertheless, this temporary reidentification of the *skene* as a specific second house is one of the harder features to parallel elsewhere in the corpus, and it is suggestive that we meet it only in Aristophanes' earliest extant play.[12]

I come finally to the play that poses by far the most numerous and difficult problems of theatrical reconstruction, and which at the very least severely tests my claim that Aristophanic spacecraft is coherent, intelligible, and consistent. *Peace* abounds in mysteries of staging: the number of doors, and the number of stage levels; the respective stage locations of Trygaeus' house, the house of Zeus, and the cave of Peace; Trygaeus' descent back to earth; and much else that I dare not broach here. Little can be said without a stand being taken on at least some of these points;[13] but clarity of the overall contours is not, I think, affected. The

---

[12] Some help may come from parallels with the comic theatricality of the Agathon scene in *Thesmophoriazusae*: there too the tragedian's home is a different space, in which interior and exterior are strongly differentiated and bridged only by an anti-illusionistic mechanism.

[13] To one persistent view I need to declare a firm antipathy: I strongly doubt that Trygaeus' house and the house of Zeus were represented by different doors. The analogy of

play is the only one to use two distinct locations at length, both in the prologue and in the body of the play, and the key spatial idea is the relationship between the two. In both the dominant theatrical idea is giving the wider community access to the divine blessings inside the stage building: first in heaven, by releasing Peace from her prison, and then on earth, by releasing one of the two attendant goddesses he brings back into the audience, and then by opening Trygaeus' own doors to all comers for the wedding feast inside as he marries the second goddess himself. Thus both the private and the public spaces are pervaded by festivity under Trygaeus' own control, and the action on earth shows the terrestrial consequences of the metaphoric, allegorical action made visible in heaven.

All this is a good deal easier to see if we appreciate the parallels, and the conventions shared, with other plays. The journey between worlds can only, as in *Frogs*, be staged in a prologue (whence the elision of the homeward journey in the parabasis). The second half of the play is built around a familiar routine, seen also in *Plutus*, *Acharnians*, and *Birds*, involving an opposition between private blessings and public aspirants mediated by the hero as gatekeeper of the *skene* door. The ending is especially close to *Ecclesiazusae*, with its civic feast offstage down an *eisodos* embodying the establishment of utopia in the wider community.

---

the *Frogs* is helpful here: the journey to heaven in *Peace* is a mirror image of the journey to the underworld in *Frogs*, where the single stage door starts out representing the house of Heracles and by the end of the journey has been reidentified as the palace of Hades. *Peace* begins and also ends its journey at Trygaeus' house on earth, but there is no reason why the door shouldn't be reidentified for the scenes in heaven in just the same way as Heracles' door is in *Frogs*. It seems quite alien to the principles of Greek staging to refocus the setting from earth to heaven and keep elements of the terrestrial setting in view (as proposed on the thesis of separate doors). In support of the more radical minority view that that the house of Zeus and the cave of Peace were the *same* door, we can also note that the cave is consistently referred to as underground, and there is in fact one other underground cave in Greek drama whose staging we can reconstruct with absolute confidence: the cave of Hermes in Sophocles' *Ichneutae*, where the cave is certainly accessed through the central stage door. The problem most widely perceived with a single-door staging is that in the heavenly half, at least, the door seems to have multiple occupants: War, Hermes, and the statue of Peace, who ought to be bumping into one another if all are using the same door. But there is a perfectly good analogy in the multiple occupants of the palace of Pluto in *Frogs*, and the solid-looking objections to a single door begin to dissolve once we start thinking in terms of how Aristophanes operates elsewhere.

The captivity of Peace in her cave recycles the opening predicament of the *Wasps*. And so on.

I have tried to show that the differences between tragic and Aristophanic spacecraft are much less than generally assumed, and can be largely explained in terms of a small set of fundamental differences between their respective spatial conventions:

| tragedy | comedy |
|---|---|
| scene-changes (almost) prohibited | scene-changes permitted (but rare, and overwhelmingly confined to prologue) |
| identity of *skene* constant | identity of *skene* flexible and sometimes anonymous |
| location established in prologue | location established in prologue or parodos |
| *Eisodoi* access terrestrial offstage spaces | *eisodoi* access terrestrial or supernal/infernal offstage spaces |
| *eisodoi* identified with opposite offstage locations | *eisodoi* not clearly distinguished |
| machinery used with restraint | machinery more casually used |
| One door only (?) | sometimes more than one door (?) |
| Location and ownership of door intertwined | location and ownership of door can be uncoupled |
| door/orchestra refocussing resisted | door/orchestra refocussing persists |

Once the implications of these differences are taken into account, Aristophanes' construction of space and spatial meaning begins to look a lot more coherent, and a lot more like that with which we are familiar in tragedy. In particular, Aristophanes shares with tragedy a strong sense of the stage door as a boundary between symbolically-opposed onstage and offstage worlds, whose precise oppositional significance can be differently constructed in different plays, but most naturally involves some kind of opposition between private interiors and public exteriors. As in tragedy, the stage space in front of the *skene* serves as a zone of contestation and mediation between the domain of the private individual or family and the wider community of the *polis* and the world outside, and the utopian plots unique to comedy exploit this spatiality as purposefully as the plots of escape and infiltration which it shares with, and perhaps derives from, tragedy and satyr-play. Though many details of staging, and even fundamental realia of comic production, remain elusive or contentious, Old Comedy's poetics of theatrical space is at least as sophisticated and resilient as that of tragedy, and deserves at least as much investment of attention.

# A little ironic, don't you think?
# Utopian criticism and the problem
# of Aristophanes' late plays

## Ian Ruffell

(University of Glasgow)

*So join the struggle while you may*
*The Revolution is just a t-shirt away*

Billy Bragg, 'Waiting for the Great Leap Forwards'[1]

Utopias, it seems, are out of fashion. From the heady and wildly misguided optimism of Mannheim in the 1930s, the dominant trend has been a suspicion of utopias as the close kin of totalitarianism. In recent times, the fall of Soviet-style Marxism has, paradoxically, precipitated a headlong adoption of Marx's own injunctions against the dangers of political utopianism. By contrast, the political culture of the early twenty-first century is widely characterised by (at best) a bland, technocratic managerialism and (at worst) a profoundly defensive attitude towards both other societies and perceived internal threats. Meanwhile technological (or economic) utopianism has been severely tempered by the dot-com bubble of the 1990s and the shattering of the illusion of a new economy; and the hopes for science, when not implicated in these explicit political and economic crises, seem to have stagnated into a glaring stand-off between a public suspicious of a scientific priesthood and a science profession dismissive of public concern. In a culture where Zamyatin's *We*, Orwell's *1984* and the various developments of the Frankenstein myth are foundational texts, it is hardly surprising that the treatment of utopianism in

---

[1] Track 11 on *Workers' Playtime* (Go! Discs, 1988).

Aristophanes and other Old Comedy has been viewed through increasingly unsympathetic lenses.

The production of Alan Sommerstein's commentaries on Aristophanes, which this volume is celebrating, has taken place in the midst of these critical and cultural developments. It is one of the manifold virtues of this series that it has always been engaged in and responsive to the academic disputes that have been raging around it.[2] Over the same period, he has also been making much more extensive interventions in these disputes, with a series of thematic articles which have dealt at greater length with the most controversial issues in Aristophanic scholarship. What we can see is an ongoing dialogue with the wider community; and, to his great credit, Sommerstein has shown himself prepared to re-evaluate his positions as part of this dialogue.

The central aim of this paper is to consider the gap between one such influential intervention, on *Ecclesiazusae* and *Wealth* (Sommerstein 1984), and the positions adopted in the final commentaries of the series, and to discuss the arguments which have led him (in part) to change or develop his position. In his original, and now classic, article, Sommerstein makes a powerful case against the then-emerging orthodoxy, which argued (and continues to argue) that the apparently utopian narratives of these last two extant Aristophanic comedies are being presented in an ironic fashion; that is to say, in crude terms, Aristophanes is in the business of criticising utopian aspirations and presenting dystopias for inspection and critique, in a manner recognizable to a reader of Orwell. This is a scenario that the Sommerstein of 1984 emphatically rejected.

> The ironic interpretation ... of *Assemblywomen* and *Wealth* cannot stand; nor can the subtler recent approaches which, while varying in the details of their analysis, all agree that Aristophanes takes a negative attitude to the sort of radical alterations of society depicted in the plays. We seem driven after all at least to entertain the possibility that a straightforward reading of the two plays is correct.
>
> (Sommerstein 1984: 332)

---

[2] I have had the chance to comment on this at some length already (Ruffell 2002). I would like once more to pay tribute to Alan Sommerstein's impressive achievement, and also to renew my call for a second edition which will give a unified account of his view of the field in the early twenty-first century.

Some fifteen years later, it is a scenario which Sommerstein now seems much more happy to entertain, at least with reference to the second of these plays, *Wealth*:

> In 391, it seems, Athens had a chance of saving herself by her exertions, in 388 it will take a miracle.
>
> (Sommerstein 2001: 22)

At the very least, this is a considerably more pessimistic reading of *Wealth* than his earlier interpretation, and as we shall see, many of the arguments of his erstwhile opponents are accepted in some form. The movement is an interesting one, and I intend to reconsider here the arguments used on both sides of the dispute. The controversy is, for good reason, particularly pointed when considering the final two plays. But the narrower dispute raises fundamental issues about how we go about analysing Old Comedy more generally. I shall be arguing, on cultural, literary and comic grounds, that both utopian and anti-utopian readings of the final plays are internally inconsistent, and rest on a number of questionable assumptions; and that an alternative reading of a complex dialogue between utopianism and anti-utopianism is not a convenient fudge which avoids the traditional question, but is actually far more consonant with the way that both comedy and ideology function.[3]

To some extent, this is revisiting and expanding some issues that were at best implicit in an earlier treatment of fragmentary utopias, not least the role of utopianism itself within an ideological framework.[4] There are three broad, related, points (contentions, assumptions or preoccupations) at the heart of my analysis. First, however much we have seen its unsavoury side in the past century, utopianism is never far from the political process. In particular, if we are to accept the compendious analysis of Ernst Bloch, his so-called "principle of hope" is an integral component of progressive politics and popular resistance to elites everywhere.[5] Indeed, utopianism has a way of re-inserting itself into the political process, even at a time such as this, which is suspicious of the concept. The first draft of this paper

---

[3] I am grateful to Ralph Rosen for pushing me on this one over a pint.

[4] Ruffell 2000.

[5] Within British political history, the example of Gerrard Winstanley and the Diggers is particularly notable, cf. Sommerstein 1984: 326 n. 75; Ruffell 2000: 480.

was written during the 2003 election campaign for the Scottish Parliament, during which (much to my surprise) I found myself turning into a political hack. As someone working in the field of political comedy, the experience was very instructive. Not least, around 15% of those who voted were attracted by species of utopianism, whether the more socialist Red or the more anarchist Green.[6]

A second consideration is that it is over-simplistic to talk of "utopias" as if it is a straightforward concept. It may well be more instructive to consider, with Marx and Bloch, utopianism and anti-utopianism as fluid principles rather than stable concepts or geographies, which it is possible to pin down typographically in anything other than very broad terms.[7] The third point is a point about comedy. It is clear especially to those involved in it (or to some of them, anyway), that Scottish (and particularly Glaswegian) politics on the left resembles nothing so much as an extended homage to Monty Python's *Life of Brian*. The serious absurdities (and ironies) of political rhetoric are a stock feature of a highly politicised landscape. In this context, it becomes critical to ask formal questions about those adjectives, ironic and serious, that continue to play such a large role in Aristophanic criticism. Rather less explicitly invoked, as a rule, but implicit in much of the discussion, are two other adjectives, logical and consistent. If logic and coherence have increasingly been questioned as the basis for Aristophanic narrative and character – and here I have in mind (though am doing less than justice to) the work of Michael Silk (Silk 1990) – and if logic and coherence stand apart from ideology, if indeed irony can be said to be constitutive of ideology,[8] then neither the ironist nor the serious positions are entirely tenable.

## *1  Irony and the Problem of the Late Plays*

Although, as I have noted, the trend of criticism of the late Aristophanic plays has tended to become extended much more readily to the comedies of the Fifth Century, the problem has historically been perceived most

---

[6] The Greens have sometimes been caricatured as millenial dystopians; but several utopian possibilities are central to Green thought. William Morris' *News from Nowhere* is perhaps the best, if highly controversial, example.

[7] For a typography of utopia, see (for example) Konstan 1990, with bibliography.

[8] On the former, see Laclau & Mouffe 2001, on the latter, Žižek 1989.

strongly in the *Ecclesiazusae* and *Wealth.*[9] But what is the problem? Clearly, these later plays are structurally distinct – being rather less fluid (or using fewer structural components) than earlier comedies – but in terms of plot structure, they do not differ so much from earlier plays such as *Acharnians* or *Birds.* But where they are perceived to be most different is in the nature of their utopian discourse. Both *Ecclesiazusae* and *Wealth* do not involve personal satisfaction or even nostalgic panhellenism, but involve a logic of social transformation, whether that is carried out by a system of legally-enacted communism under the aegis of politically powerful women or consists of the divinely-inspired redistribution of *Wealth.* It is this social transformation that critics – with the conspicuous exception of Alan Sommerstein – have found difficult to swallow.

And this is a mark of his academic honesty, because the logic of his interpretative strategy has led him to create a late Aristophanes that is the antithesis of his early Aristophanes. Taking a strongly biographical approach to criticism, Sommerstein follows de Ste. Croix (1972) in seeing the Aristophanes of Athens' period of power as essentially a social conservative, and the Aristophanes of early Fourth-Century Athens as someone committed to social reform. Just as he explains the stylistic and structural changes in biographical terms as evidence of the declining powers of old age (1984: 314), so too is the perceived ideological shift explained in biographical terms: as horror at the exigencies that have been forced on the Attic peasantry post-Peloponnesian War, horror perhaps at the excesses of the Thirty, disillusionment with the *kaloikagathoi* (1984: 332–3). Put crudely, then, Aristophanes has become a class traitor. If I find the biographical criticism not to my taste, and by any standards the personal shift takes a lot of swallowing, this does have the conspicuous virtue of interpretative consistency, at least at the level of methodology.

By contrast, in 2000, Sommerstein has begun to waver on his defiant interpretation of *Wealth.* The anti-ironic rhetoric does continue. And certainly, he continues to maintain (for the most part) the logical and ethical integrity of Chremylus' character and his plan, one of the key points at dispute. He argues that the end result mirrors (and justifies)

---

[9] Zimmermann 1983; Heberlein 1981; Schwinge 1977; Flashar 1967.

Chremylus' original goals, and follows Rogers' interpretation that in *Wealth* everyone becomes rich and virtuous.[10] Nonetheless he has begun to accept many of the arguments and critical principles of the ironic camp (if it may be put in those terms). Most notably, he accepts that Chremylus comes off badly in the central debate, where his plans for universal riches are subjected to the harsh scrutiny of Poverty, Penia (415–626). Penia, according to this view, is the repository of critical, logical analysis and Chremylus is forced to resort to emotional outbursts and violence to overcome her (something of a come-down from his earlier good intentions). With perhaps the conspicuous exception of James McGlew 1997, this has been the consensus of most modern critics.[11]

Furthermore, the very lack of realism in the plan itself is now also developed as a cause for downplaying the force or commitment of *Wealth*. Thus, according to Sommerstein's current view, if the utopia of *Ecclesiazusae* is theoretically possible (though arguably never achieved in practice), it is meant seriously, but because the goal of *Wealth* requires divine assistance, it is expressing the futility of fantasy.

By acknowledging in *Wealth* the problematic aspects of the plausibility of the protagonist's plan, the means by which it is put into practice, the character of the protagonist, and the strength of the dissenting voices, Sommerstein is making greater concessions than he is prepared to admit. In 1984, he resists giving way on any of these grounds, for as he must have seen they affect his interpretation of *Ecclesiazusae* as much as *Wealth*. And if we can analyze *Ecclesiazusae* in these terms, then why not *Birds* or *Acharnians*? Thus indeed are the very arguments that have developed over the last couple of decades.[12]

It is, I think, unfortunate that Sommerstein should have given way here. Although as I shall argue, some movement is necessary, these particular points are not perhaps the ones he should have let go. We can see similar tensions in his 1998 edition of *Ecclesiazusae*. Here, Sommerstein is again

---

[10] See Sommerstein 2001: 14–15, 18; cf. Rogers 1907 on line 430.

[11] So, recently, Bowie 1993: 284–291, Olson 1990. Even McGlew sidesteps a number of the issues by seeing the play as being primarily about promoting the collective power of fantasy. *Ecclesiazusae* has fared somewhat better than *Wealth*, with Slater 2002: 207–234 and Ober 1999: 122–155 offering positive readings, although the latter, in particular, does not seem to address the heart of the ironic case. See further below.

[12] See, for example, Bowie 1993; Hubbard 1991.

very concerned with questions of practical success and failure, and seeks to attain consistency between Praxagora's plan and actual outcomes. Nonetheless, we can see the same type of concessions, but also some special pleading employed to cover it. Thus questions of practicality are again an issue (Sommerstein 1998: 20). He accepts that 'the Dissident' has the last word with his planned evasion of Praxagora's regime. A choral ode is hypothesized in order to serve this answering function (Sommerstein 1998: 20–1, and on 875). In particular he sees the exploration of sexuality in 877–1111 not as a comic debunking of the arrogance of youth (Sommerstein 1984: 320–1), but as a genuinely disturbing scene (Sommerstein 1998: 21–2). This is explained away as a 'parenthesis' to satisfy the male audience members' expectations of *gunaikokratia*. However, the emphasis on practical success and failure is somewhat at odds with a rather different strand of argument which stresses rather more the disjunction between the fantastic, impossible plot and the real critique of underlying issues.

It is this approach that can begin to open up the entire framing of the debate between the ironists and non-ironists. The terms of this debate, which have hitherto been broadly agreed by both sides, are what I am particularly concerned with here. Both sides privilege realism, coherence and logic, and in particular use these tools to assess the protagonist, his plan and their respective outcomes. In its classic form, the debate between ironists and non-ironists is whether one side can undermine the claims of (above all) *Ecclesiazusae* and *Wealth* in these terms, and as such the debate is strongly binary, a flipping from non-ironic to ironic, from black to white.

It would be misleading, however, to represent this as an opposition between the ironic and the serious. In contrast to those who take the view that comedy has no (need of) political reference or impact, that it need not have any strong meaning or ideological intervention but that it is mainly played for laughs alone,[13] the two major camps, both the modern ironists and the non-ironists, are committed to a serious, strongly historicized and for the most part an intentionalist view of comedy. But in fact the ironists are engaged in still more of a leap than those who are unambiguously

---

[13] So Dover 1972, Ussher 1973.

attached to a surface meaning. The problem is: should a loss of coherence, or the presence of one or more strong alternative voices lead us to interpret the play as an attack on the central idea, its proponent or the comic world that has been created? This is, to say the least, a strong interpretative leap to make.

If, however, irony is simply a supposedly obvious reversal of the surface meaning, in crude terms laughing at rather than with, this is no easier to control than a straightforward meaning and arguably much, much harder. A cause célèbre in the history of British sit-com is Johnny Speight's *Till Death Us Do Part, In Sickness and in Health* and their various spin-offs, featuring the bigot Alf Garnett.[14] As is well-known (and indeed, this made it into my entry-level sociology textbook at school), both the writer and the lead actor, Warren Mitchell, have claimed frequently that this was meant to be a satire on the racist, sexist and homophobic bigotry espoused by the central figure and that the offence this caused was a mistake. But I remember at the time finding the claims that it was not meant seriously deeply odd. For all the audiences that I encountered in deepest Essex found in Alf Garnett a figure with which to identify, at least partially – sometimes in the sense of a sympathetic, "Oh, isn't he dreadful", but essentially a figure that reinforced existing prejudice.[15]

Are we forced then to posit two audiences, of the cognoscenti and the illiterate, the educated and the oiks, the few and the many, and say that the genuine meaning is – as Angus Bowie puts it – only there "if they have eyes to see" (1993: 291). Or, to put it another way, is the non-ironic reading of Alf Garnett an instance of mass, aberrant decoding? And if that repugnant figure can be read straight, can we really be confident that (generally less outspoken, but perhaps ideologically more unsettling) Aristophanic characters were not too? It is true that there are some grounds for seeing such a divide in Aristophanes himself – not so much through his collective indictment of the audience in *Clouds* and its aftermath for failing

---

[14] Archie Bunker in the US remake, *All in the Family*.

[15] The reception of *Till Death Us Do Part* is considerably complicated by its two long runs, its spin-offs and its return in the 1980s. Tony Booth, who played the left-wing son-in-law in the first series, argues that there was a shift from unsettling taboo-breaking at the very start towards something much more cosy, with a royal command performance and approval from the Queen Mother (Booth 2002: 116–122). For some analysis of the show, see Ross 1996.

to be intelligent (δεξιοὺς, 521), wise (σοφοῖς, 535) or sensible (εὖ φρονεῖν, 562), which clearly denotes a collective failure to appreciate his self-evident genius (or so he claims), but above all through his bid for victory at the end of the *Ecclesiazusae*:

σμικρὸν δ᾽ ὑποθέσθαι τοῖς κριταῖσι βούλομαι·
τοῖς σοφοῖς μὲν τῶν σοφῶν μεμνημένοις κρίνειν ἐμέ,
τοῖς γελῶσι δ᾽ ἡδέως διὰ τὸν γέλων κρίνειν ἐμέ –
σχεδὸν ἅπαντας οὖν κελεύω δηλαδὴ κρίνειν ἐμέ –
μηδὲ τὸν κλῆρον γενέσθαι μηδὲν ἡμῖν αἴτιον,
ὅτι προείληχ᾽·

There's a small suggestion I want to make to the judges:
that whoever's clever remembers the clever stuff and votes for me,
that whoever's laughing enjoys the jokes and votes for me –
yes, clearly that's almost all of you I'm telling to vote for me –
and not let the ballot influence our result,
the one about the order of play we took earlier.          *Eccl.* 1154–1159

However, in none of these cases do we seem to be dealing with interpretative strategies, so much as subject-matter (crudely, serious issues versus knob gags, or so he would have us believe). Moreover, from the audience's point of view, it is perfectly possible (indeed, I would suggest, probable) that they would perceive the crucial adjective and participle phrases as denoting roles or strategies rather than identities. There is, of course, nothing to prevent someone from being clever and laughing at the same time. This does not help us to posit such a bifurcated audience as it at first sight appears.[16]

To return to the problem of ironic decoding, I would myself prefer (at the least) to build in a reader-response element if I were to assess the interpretation of *Till Death Us Do Part*. More precisely, I would want to see both the ironic and the non-ironic interpretation activating elements that are in the performance – precisely what impact those have on the audience, reinforcing, undermining or shocking existing sensibilities, is going to depend largely on their context (class, gender, ethnicity), their political beliefs and the nature of their personal dispositions. It is

---

[16] Sommerstein himself comes close to this position (1998: 22), identifying the two strands as riotous comic triumph plus serious moral aspect.

interesting to note, however, that in a suburban, lower-middle-class context, attraction to the views of the inner-city working-class Tory, Alf Garnett (as indeed to those of his upper-class, erstwhile-classicist alter ego, Enoch Powell), was based neither on liking of the character nor on similar education, nor on any class solidarity, so much as ideological affinity. Whether that production represented a colossal miscalculation or cynical manipulation on the part of the author is a matter of debate (although I incline to the latter). What is not in dispute is that the series aggressively problematised contemporary issues through a voice that was not representing in any straightforward sense either orthodoxy or opposition. If irony is itself problematic and I have reservations about simple binaries,

I have still deeper reservations about the underlying categories and assumptions that are invoked in this debate, with their emphasis on coherence and consistency, and their essentially teleological aspect. I have already mentioned the plausibility and coherence of the opening plan. To this we may add the coherence and consistency of the central character's objectives throughout the play; the extent to which their ideas are effectively challenged; and the extent to which the objectives are shown to have succeeded. (What constitutes 'succeeded' is of course up for grabs.) The emphasis on character often has a distinctly ethical air – and so for example Sommerstein is concerned to ensure that Chremylus remains ethical and (above all) unselfish. The selfishness (or not) of the central characters is a recurring feature in the secondary literature (but above all perhaps in respect of the *Acharnians*).[17] But even more than with beliefs over what constitutes plausibility, the critics' own beliefs over what constitutes virtue can be rather variable.

The plausibility of a scenario, and in particular the nature or success of the schemes of the protagonist is, I suggest, no means – or at least a poor means – to measure the ideological manipulations of a comic plot. It might be objected at this point that this is a straw man with which to berate fellow critics. However, I point to one of the most recent in-depth studies of the play, by Douglas Olson, which bases an ironic reading of *Wealth* around the central, to him surprising, finding that:

> Although it is gratifying ... this is in no sense a coherent prescription for concrete political change. (Olson 1990: 232)

---

[17] See, for example, Foley 1988 and Bowie 1988 and the response of Parker 1991.

And there was me thinking that this is where major political thinkers had gone wrong, by failing to follow the plot-lines of Old Comedy. Of course the main plot of *Wealth* is not a viable prescription in any literal sense (any more than personal peaces or cities in the air). My point here is that the non-literal senses are always the ones we should be worrying about. And to follow one cheap shot with another, consider, for example, a modern analogy. It makes as much sense as assessing the contribution of *South Park: Bigger, Longer and Uncut* to debates on censorship through an assessment of, variously, the realism of its animation, the likelihood of the death penalty for bad language (even by the concerned parents of deepest Colorado), the probability that the Canadian Air Force would bomb the Baldwin family as a political reprisal, or the plausibility that four eight-year-olds would try to rescue prisoners from the tender mercies of the US Army (with or without the assistance of a refugee from film noir). The list could go on.

What is the alternative? It seems to me that the best we can do is to embrace the multi-stranded nature of the discourse and to resist the temptation to boil things down to a simple position. In terms of the late plays of Aristophanes, this is something that has been developed most effectively by Konstan and Dillon back in the 80s, in their reading of *Wealth*. Although they operate under the assumption that a work of literature is striving towards unity, and effectively buy into an optimistic surface trajectory as an Aristophanic goal, they unpick the contradictions in order to reveal the overdetermined nature of the ideological structures beneath. As a piece of structural Marxist criticism,[18] this is very instructive. But I would want to question that comedy is 'covering up' the gaps, heedless of the rather conspicuous contradictions, and instead suggest that it is posing a very sharp dialogue that is exploiting that ideological overdetermination, pursuing hits on both sides. This probably sounds like a familiar, dialogic, Bakhtinian shtick, and yes it probably is. However, I would further suggest that a structural tension between plausiblity/implausibility, concrete/imaginary and logic/illogic is integral both to humour and the potential for critique through comedy. If I am keeping multiple balls in the air, I do also want to suggest that some are

---

[18] They explicitly base their position on that of Macherey 1978.

bigger than others – and that Alan Sommerstein's defence of Chremylus and Praxagora is not necessarily the one (if any) that should be dropped.

## 2  *Philosophy and Rhetoric in the Late Plays*

The critical debates around Aristophanes thus privilege logic and coherence within a simple binary, but evaluation of the status of speakers and their opinions is a problem of ideology, not logic. And as writers on ideology have insisted, ideologies are not logical, but complex and overdetermined – and this far I would walk up the Althusserian path.[19] In the case of *Wealth* and *Ecclesiazusae*, however, the problems of logic are still more problematic, as the status of philosophy and logic themselves is at the heart of the debate. In the case of *Wealth*, an ironic approach to utopianism involves the privileging of philosophical ideas; in *Ecclesiazusae* an ironic reading requires a reading that satirises philosophical ideas that are held to lie beneath it. Although I would hate to say that comedy cannot opportunistically use any discourse to hand, the ironic reading in particular requires a radically different approach to the same discourse within the same period.[20] In the first play (it might be and has been suggested), it is Praxagora's espousal of the utopian philosophical dream of the ideal state that is being set up as ridiculous – that is to say, Praxagora is being set up as the butt of the humour because of the nature of her schemes. In the second play (it is suggested), it is the devastating critique of Chremylus' plans by Penia that shows how his plans are in any literal sense impossible and thus to be mocked. Penia's critique is intellectual, to be set against the emotional promptings of Chremylus.

The philosophical ideas are not, however, to be considered in isolation. It is striking that both purveyors of these ideas are women and need to be considered within the gender politics of the day. The utopian schemes, their proposers and their opponents need to be interpreted against this context. Here, it seems clear that Penia pushes buttons in the masculine mindset that are not so clearly activated in the case of Praxagora.

---

[19] Althusser 1969, 1971.

[20] A more positive reading of *Ecclesiazusae* does not require the foregrounding of philosophical discourse in the same way as the ironic.

Curiously, critics have tended to see Praxagora as the figure whose schemes are undermined by her gender, not Penia. I would claim precisely the opposite, that (even more than in *Lysistrata*, which it echoes), *Ecclesiazusae* presents Praxagora in such a way as to render the implausible plausible.

## 2.1 The Paradoxes of Praxagora

Of the three versions of *gunaikokratia* in the extant plays, it is *Ecclesiazusae* that is the most edgy. The explicit focus of the play on issues of social reform makes the disruptive nature of the protagonist and her allies all the more striking and potentially threatening. Much more than in *Lysistrata*, the women engage in the masculine political sphere. Rather than a *coup d' état* and the exploitation of sacred space as in *Lysistrata*, and retiring gracefully after restoring panhellenic harmony, the women of *Ecclesiazusae* strike out here explicitly into the world of the assembly and maintain that politically central position. If the pitch for men is that they will be looked after in the new set-up, their loss of political power is absolute. It is true that Praxagora herself disappears from view once the new state has been established, but the claims of women under the new dispensation do not – indeed, they are notoriously part of the problem for critics, as we shall see. All the same, given the social and political context, it is hardly surprising that the play does emphasize the effect on / contrast with male citizens. And if the fact that these are social and political reforms makes the issue of women's status more pressing, so too the fact that it is women engineering the social reform reflects on the nature and status of that social reform.

For many critics, the topsy-turvy element dominates all, and over-whelms the claims of the social reform and the social reformer. That it is a woman who is the agent for these new-fangled ideas fatally undermines their plausibility. So Bernhard Zimmermann claims that identity of the heroine, together with the representation of men within the audience, posed an insurmountable obstacle for the audience.

> Der Hauptheld ist eine Frau, mit der sich das männliche Publikum nicht ohne weiteres identifizieren konnte, zumal die Männer im Stück nicht gerade in glanzvollem Licht erscheinen.

> The chief hero is a woman, with whom the male citizens could not
> identify without a second thought, especially as the men in the play do
> not exactly appear in a lustrous light.
>
> (Zimmermann 1983: 74)

Others, while less categorical, have pursued a similarly bifurcated
approach. The irruption of the feminine aspect of the *oikos* into the
masculine aspect of public space, and the redefinition of that masculine
space in feminine terms, is problematic. While not wishing to minimize the
shock value of what the men are seeing, albeit considerably eased by the
intertextual heritage of the play, I do want to suggest that in a much more
fundamental way than *Lysistrata*, *Ecclesiazusae* exploits paradoxical
aspects of the status of women in such a way as to destabilise reality, but
also retain a grip on and potential reference to it. In other words, κωμῳδία
here is exploiting the paradoxical and over-coded nature of ideology
itself.[21] Against Zimmermann's diagnosis of this social disruption as
'distancing' and 'illusion-breaking'.[22] It will be clear, however, that I am
suggesting much more a logic of ideological implication and embedding –
manipulation from within.

The position of women within that system is itself one of the most
ambivalent aspects. If they are, in a formal sense, not citizens, in Athens
nonetheless they are necessary for the religious dimension of civic life; but
they are also the subject of extensive regulations that secure Athenian
citizenship in men, and as such have a para-citizen rôle themselves. This
ambivalence is one reason why *gunaikokratia* is a productive source for
the generation of alternative realities that are nonetheless ideologically
proximate to the ones left behind.[23] In *Lysistrata*, the civic duties within
the religious sphere were emphasised – and that is whether or not we
include contemporary priestesses as possible referents for the central
characters (and my own feeling is that we should). Although in
*Ecclesiazusae* the religious element is not neglected, coming most

---

[21] See especially Laclau & Mouffe 2001.

[22] cf. Zimmermann 1983: 74 n. 78. This is sloppy use of the term, especially when the
metatheatrical performance of gender is such a feature of the play, on which see Taaffe
1993 and, most recently, Slater 2002.

[23] For comparison of *gunaikokratia* with the ideological problem of the non-slave
utopia, see Vidal-Naquet 1986.

conspicuously in the mock Panathenaia,[24] it is the citizenship angle proper that is explored. If Praxagora is as exceptional as Lysistrata in terms of her public speaking, her background is much more clearly articulated – and shows that potentially anyone can learn how to engage in politics.

Whereas Lysistrata belatedly articulates her claims to political knowledge in terms of explicit male pedagogy and the rather ambivalent authority of a parody of Euripides (*Lys.* 1124–7), Praxagora is self-taught, and with particular reference to public speaking at the assembly, her being in a position to learn follows directly from the mismanagement of the Peloponnesian War by the men.

> ἐν ταῖς φυγαῖς μετὰ τἀνδρὸς ᾤκησ' ἐν Πυκνί.
> ἔπειτ' ἀκούουσ' ἐξέμαθον τῶν ῥητόρων.

> In the refugee-camps, I lived with my husband on the Pnyx.
> It was then that I learned, listening to the politicians.
> *Ecclesiazusae* 243–4

It's not clear exactly to which population-displacements these φυγαῖς refer – the best candidates being the movement from the Attic countryside during the Archidamian War (and/or after the Spartans had fortified Deceleia).[25] What does seem clear is that the opportunity to learn is implicated within normal political practice, and the results of that practice. It might have been possible to dismiss Praxagora as a temporary aberration, the product of extreme circumstances, which could be solved by a return to some pre-lapsarian status, were it not for warfare and such results as Praxagora's being a near-constant of Athenian life, certainly over the previous forty years, and ones that Aristophanes and his colleagues laid at the door of all politicians from Perikles to Kleophon. All this serves to undermine (or at least to complicate extensively) the problems presented by Praxagora to an Athenian audience. Moreover, despite the problems that she has in sharing this knowledge with her comrades, which does plug

---

[24] *Ecclesiazusae* 730–745, with comments below, cf. *Lysistrata* 638–647. See also *Eccl.* 223a on the maintenance of the Thesmophoria.

[25] An alternative is the period from the fall to the restoration of the democracy, although that would seem to imply an end to regular political activity.

into the standard repertoire of misogyny, nonetheless within the world of the play they are in fact ultimately and collectively successful. This is contrasted with male failure – to borrow from Michael Moore, the defeat of Athens is on this argument being ascribed to stupid white men.

The extent to which Praxagora and her friends exploit the complex – and potentially paradoxical – nature of Athenian ideology is perhaps best seen in the field of gender relations. For it is not simply the case that the women can (in part) perform as politicians, or even that they can play men more generally – and again *Ecclesiazusae* dramatises this in a much less hedged way than earlier plays – but also that male roles are pushing the limits of what a Foucauldian logic could sustain. The women's coup is happening when the most powerful, capable and/or effective politicians are occupying theoretically subordinate positions .

   καὶ πῶς γυναικῶν θηλύφρων ξυνουσία
   δημηγορήσει;

Πρ. πολὺ μὲν οὖν ἄριστά που.
   λέγουσι γὰρ καὶ τῶν νεανίσκων ὅσοι
   πλεῖστα σποδοῦνται, δεινοτάτους εἶναι λέγειν·
   ἡμῖν δ᾽ ὑπάρχει τοῦτο κατὰ τύχην τινά.

  And how is it that a gathering of women, thinking in feminine ways, will
  be public speakers?

Prax. As for that, better than anyone by far.
   For they reckon that all the young men
   who have been screwed most deeply, are the most brilliant speakers.
   And that's just our thing– as luck would have it!

                   *Ecclesiazusae* 110–114

The pattern of *Clouds* seems to be confirmed, and Athens looks to be fucked. But this can't be dismissed as a topsy-turvy aberration, a temporary case of Kleisthenes being in charge of the asylum. Not only does the entire political class – or at least the effective political class – appear to occupy this position, but (as becomes clear) the alternative models of masculinity on offer in the play only seem to reinforce the paradox of the Foucauldian paradigm, when the Other has become the top. Praxagora's understanding of the paradoxes that surround or derive from a Foucauldian zero-sum game is all too clear. The simple binary of fucker and fucked becomes problematic when the category of fucked is held to include all those most capable of learning rhetoric and philosophy. Praxagora's observation is that if you are going to lump everyone Other together in a binary fashion, the "logic" (so-called) is precisely that the rest of the Other should have a crack of the whip. Or, once power has been conceded to the passive Other, then the overload on the paradoxes starts creaking. Indeed, as she argues, the women's experience and consistency in playing the role of the Other leaves them even better placed than these amateur Athenian fledglings like Agyrrhios (102–3). Disentangling the complications involve a long, hard look at the ideological underpinnings of sex and gender.

There are, of course, further paradoxes. The powerfully passive women are also representatives of τὸν ἀρχαῖον νόμον (216), even as they embark upon a revolution. But this is no simple nostalgia – or, better, the complications of nostalgia provide the potential for their revolution. This is neither a particularly moral *nomos* – at least given the usual stereotypes of women in comedy, which are all retailed for the delectation of the audience (224–8) – nor is it at all consistent with what passes for *nomos* with the men: thus Praxagora's criticism of the Athenian tendency to change and innovation.

> κοὐχὶ μεταπειρωμένας
> ἴδοις ἂν αὐτάς· ἡ δ' Ἀθηναίων πόλις,
> εἰ τοῦτο χρηστῶς εἶχεν, οὐκ ἂν ἐσῴζετο,
> εἰ μή τι καινόν γ' ἄλλο περιηργάζετο.

> ...and as for changing the practice, you wouldn't see the women do that.
> But the city of Athens,
> if the thing were sorted, wouldn't keep it that way,
> if it couldn't be messing around with some innovation instead.
>
> *Ecclesiazusae* 217–220

On the other hand, though, her argument is that "if it ain't broke, don't fix it"; but it is broke and needs fixing. The striking thing is that the opportunity for a simple nostalgic solution is emphatically denied here. Indeed, the reinforcing of τὸν ἀρχαῖον νόμον with the emphatic mantra of "just as before" (ὥσπερ καὶ πρὸ τοῦ, 221–8) suggests that it is the impulse to nostalgia as well as to innovation that is being questioned. It is not so long since terrible things were done in the name of some "ancestral constitution". Of course if you take an ironic line, then it is nostalgia that is itself problematic; but the argument – and the humour – seems to be considerably more complicated than that, exploiting the complicated status of nostalgia. Nostalgia is problematic, but it is also the case that the lack of nostalgia – or is it just the lack of history – is problematic.

The final, major paradox, is the collapsing of the metaphor of the *polis* as *oikos*. Here, as Helene Foley has insisted,[26] the dialectic is complex, and cannot simply be addressed in terms of a simple opposition between masculine *polis* and feminine *oikos*. The point that I want to stress is that it is the pervasiveness with which the *polis* was seen in terms of the *oikos* that increases the plausibility of the women's scheme. For this we can look at Aristotle's treatment of κοινωνίαι in the *Politics* (esp. Bk. I) – and here his definition of the *polis* as the *telos* of such communities and as prior to mankind is his own controversialist position.[27] But we can also look at Aristophanic drama, most obviously *Knights*, for the exploration of this metaphor. And if this metaphor is one that readily structured the conception of the *polis*, it is striking too that Praxagora, like Lysistrata before her (and the intertext is striking), is given arguments that stem directly from women's expertise within the *oikos*: wool-working (the female *tekhne* par excellence, cf. 215–7, *Lys.* 567–586) and above all the management of household resources and accounts (211–12, *Lys.* 493–5). Both plays use arguments that (within context) derive from women's expertise but talk directly to metaphors that shape the dominant (masculine) ideology. However, the ability to draw intertextually on an earlier powerful and successful character, is something that is, of course, only available to the later play.

Thus I would suggest that *Ecclesiazusae* is concerned both to ramp up the plausibility of its implausible protagonist, but does so in a way that opens up questions, rather than closing them down. It is not, however, the character of Praxagora that ultimately drives the kernel of ironic readings, which as I have suggested tend to focus (like management) on aims and outcomes. Even here, though, more questions are raised than answered. Consider first the infamous conjunctions in both *Ecclesiazusae* and *Wealth* of sex and the city. Of the outcomes of Praxagora's plans, it is the interruption of the romantic interlude by randy old women that has caused

---

[26] Foley 1982.
[27] The authoritarian implications of this are explored by Taylor 1995.

most opprobrium from the critics (and not just the male critics, either). The horror! I have to confess that I have always found it rather hard to feel sorry for either of the lovelorn couple at this point. This may just mean that I am just a hardened anti-romantic; on the other hand, I worry that we are importing too many notions of romantic love into this scene. Yes the old women are presented as monstrous, but I think we need to look hard at the apparent alternative. It is worth considering the somewhat parallel developments in *Wealth*; there, too, the old woman receives a fearful amount of abuse from both her ex-toyboy and from Chremylus; but nonetheless the young man is presented as a thoroughly nasty piece of work and does not come off scot-free (1084–8, cf. 1200–4). The abuse is double-handed and the outcome not one-sided.

There is more going on in *Ecclesiazusae* than merrily satirising both young love and ancient desperation. As Douglas Olson (1988) has shown, the extensive parody here suggests that the cheesy conventions of lyric poetry are as much up for grabs in this scene as an assault on the dignity of the Old Women, though assuredly it does the latter too. Rather more subtly, as he has shown, the lyric that the young man and young woman sing (952–975b) enacts the new world order, as they intertwine different aspects of active and passive lovers in a parodic reworking of a *paraclausithyron* narrative. So the story that the Old Women interrupt and disrupt is not even the conventional order of things. Indeed, if we are looking to the social (rather than intertextual) order, which is where so many critical narratives do look, and even allowing for the parodied passionate froth and for the comic stereotype of women, it is not clear that a young man ought to be enticing an unmarried young woman to open the door to him. The gap between poetry and reality is already one of the ideological conflicts at stake here. Part of the joke, surely, is that communal love, at least in this formulation, is not a free-for-all, in which everyone is a winner and sexual expression free. Indeed, the role that the older women play here in policing this youthful expression of sexuality might be seen in some sense as analogous to the policing of sexual roles under the previous dispensation (by older women or by others), and placing that policing as much under the microscope as their own behaviour under Praxagora's republic.[28]

We can, I think, go further. I suggested earlier that their ambivalent status, as non-citizen guarantors of male economic and civic status, is what made women so productive for comedy. It is striking that the conjunction of economic and sexual rights of the citizen should return with a vengeance in the duet scene. Although it is often shown how much this scene is a critique of communal sexuality, what has not been seen is that this derives primarily from the already-existing male analogues. If marriage between older men and younger women was rather less objectionable to male eyes (as indeed in most patriarchal cultures), there was one area in Athens where this kind of relationship was particularly anxious and critical – the *epikleros*. Her legally-hedged and regulated status was a guarantor of the *oikos* and *polis* intertwined, and leveraged the ambiguous citizen status of the woman involved. What we can see here, I suggest, is not so much a reversal as an extension of this most economic of civic interventions featuring within this new marriage of *oikos* and *polis*. If a fresh look at the *polis* as *oikos* raises questions about economic and social justice in material terms, if it is posing the problem of the relationship between economic and civic participation, then those questions cannot but spread into the ideological structures of gender within which they are just as heavily implicated.[29]

### 2.2 The Poverty of Philosophy

I have cheerfully been avoiding the question so far of whether there were actually in existence any such developed utopian ideas in circulation at the time of *Ecclesiazusae*, that is to say that through the figure of Praxagora, Aristophanes is working against some Platonic precursors (such as Phaleas of Chalcedon), or some early Platonic musings, or whether Aristophanes is picking up and running with much more nascent ideas. I myself would like

---

[28] Recently, Slater 2002: 224–5 has shown himself to be less than swayed by the youth, on the grounds of dereliction of duty, but rather sweepingly claims that these lyrics have a "simple dramatic purpose" and "need not detain us".

[29] I owe much here to comments by Chloe Stewart.

to retain some scope here for the imaginative contribution of comedy,[30] but whatever their source Praxagora is punting some radical, intellectual ideas, which contradict established logic and custom. Nonetheless, care is taken to ramp up her plausibility. The same could not be said of Penia in *Wealth*, indeed the very opposite is the case. The ironic thing is that the prize exhibit in ironic readings of *Wealth* is supposedly the devastating critique that she offers of the plans of Chremylus, from an apparently similar font of intellectual innovation. But whereas Penia's 'truth' is from the start presented as counter-intuitive and unpalatable, critics have rushed to applaud. And I am very confused. Dare we see the ideological bias of the academy here?

As we shall see the ideas of Penia are just as strikingly radical and uncomfortable as those of Praxagora, but in stark contrast to the sober-sided matron of the *Ecclesiazusae* (and her precursor from Lysistrata), Penia has the book of male anxiety thrown at her. She is presented visually as a Fury, with a demeanour to match.[31] Blepsidemos and Chremylus, in their horrified reaction (423–5), conjure up an intertextual tragic heritage of violence, blood-feuding and revenge, not to mention the persecution of representatives of the masculine cultural order.[32]

Χρ.    σὺ δ' εἶ τίς; ὠχρὰ μὲν γὰρ εἶναί μοι δοκεῖς.
Βλ.    ἴσως Ἐρινύς ἐστιν ἐκ τραγῳδίας·
          βλέπει γέ τοι μανικόν τι καὶ τραγῳδικόν.
Χρ.    ἀλλ' οὐκ ἔχει γὰρ δᾷδας.
Βλ.                                        οὐκοῦν κλαύσεται.

---

[30] That Aristophanes influenced Plato is strongly argued by Sommerstein 1998: 13–17, although that does not rule out Aristophanes developing more purely economic ideas of earlier theorists.

[31] On the significance of the visual dimension of Penia, see McGlew 1997: 37–8.

[32] Sommerstein rules out a reference to the *Oresteia* here on the grounds that torches are not explicitly mentioned as attributes of the Furies, but this does not seem to me to be a good reason to exclude this play from the audience's horizon of expectations. It misses both the possibility of creative revivals and the intertextual weight the *Eumenides* could carry as a key literary supplier of the Furies' character. Moreover, the torchlit procession of the *Eumenides* 1003–1047 is a striking association of the two, even if the Furies are not the ones holding the items themselves.

Chrem. Who are you?  You're looking pallid to me.
Bleps.  Perhaps she's a Fury from tragedy.
        She certainly looks mad and has the tragic look.
Chrem. Well, she's got no torches.
Bleps.                                    In that case, she's going to scream.

*Wealth* 422–5

While Praxagora subtly detonates the overcoding of ideological structures by operating from within, this supposed voice of Sophistic reason is aggressively confrontational and oppositional, contained within a body of a demon, an intertext of unthinking revenge and the male fear of uncontrolled nature. This is certainly not to diminish the paradoxical nature of Praxagora, but as a mainstay of at least the first two-thirds of the play, her character is much more subtle than the violent irrationality of the rational Penia. So for the latter to be the carrier of the ironic key, this is, to say the least, odd. Even without the comparison with Praxagora, the disjunction between what Penia says and how she looks, acts and is described is odd, paradoxical and, of course, very funny.

Let us then turn to the debate between Chremylus and Penia. To recap, Chremylus' argument is quite simply that the curing of Ploutos, so that he can spot the virtuous ones who deserve riches, will lead to everyone becoming good and (thus) rich and also respecting τὰ θεῖα (489–497). This last one is interesting, since Chremylus makes it plain that the current state of affairs is liable to be viewed as the manifestation of divine ill-will (501). Penia counters by claiming that if Chremylus' dream becomes reality, then everything will fall apart – there will be no motivation for work and no need for trade. Production of luxury artefacts will cease, and there will be need for everyone after all to pursue their own crafts. In effect, magical acquisition of Wealth will annihilate the economy (507–516).

As has been well advertised, Chremylus responds to the arguments of Penia with threats rather than reasoned argument. He threatens physical force from the beginning and responds to her argument about thrift with a wish for it to rebound on her (527), likewise he ends a dispute over mythological exempla with a further threat (592). Finally, of course, he sends Penia packing with at the very least a flea in her ear, and probably something rather more solid. And, horror of horrors, he maintains that he will never, ever, be persuaded.

ἀλλὰ φθείρου καὶ μὴ γρύξῃς
   ἔτι μηδ' ὁτιοῦν.
   οὐ γὰρ πείσεις, οὐδ' ἢν πείσῃς.

Get lost – and don't grizzle

another single thing.
You won't persuade me, not even if you persuade me.

*Wealth* 599–600

Critics have been happy to see this as damning evidence that Chremylus has lost the intellectual case – and he knows it.[33] But I think that we can provide good motivation for Chremylus, even if we can't necessarily excuse this lapse into violent direct action. This culmination of the dispute provides a good starting point for this rehabilitation. The repetition of πείθω suggests that it is rhetorical skill as well as the intellectual force of Penia's argument that is at stake here, perhaps in addition the idea that the verbal picture conjured up by the character does not match material reality. In the stakes of sophism, Chremylus is for the most part not a high roller; Penia, by contrast has both the moves and the material.

Penia is the personification of a sophistic argument. She is, in a sense, the arguing of a controversy made flesh. As has been pointed out, she seeks to teach Chremylus as an ignorant student (473, 477).[34] And she seeks to fight the argument on the grounds of economics and politics rather than wish-fulfilment. In that sense, she would be better off tackling a harder case like Praxagora – or Plato. Chremylus by contrast is a soft, almost irrelevant target, at least in philosophical terms. This suggests perhaps that we are not meant to be concentrating on Chremylus – no Five Year Planner, but seeking a miraculous Great Leap Forward – but that we are rather supposed to be paying attention to the arguments of Penia. And clearly she is presented as someone at home in the academy. That her argument for what is presented as (to Blepsidemos and Chremylus) a difficult, unexpected or contentious position of principle is reminiscent of the sophists, in everything from *Clouds* to Gorgias' *Helen* via Antiphon's *Tetralogies*; while we may also note that her emphasis on crafts, τέχναι (510–516, esp. 511; 534), is reminiscent of Socratic and other early-fourth

---

[33] This is one of the areas where Sommerstein has given way (2001: 19).
[34] cf. McGlew 1997: 40.

century philosophical discourse. Moreover, as her defenders point out, her arguments are prototypes for political economists, from Aristotle onwards, if not earlier.[35] Such theories are not the core concerns of most of the population of the period or indeed of most comic (especially comic utopian) discourse of the period.

Rather more significant are the dubious arguments she adduces in order to assert positively her own status. These rely on some staggeringly hair-splitting distinctions, not least in seeking to distinguish herself, noble Poverty, from Beggary (548). Under questioning, even Penia herself seems to admit to concede that popularly there was close kinship between them (550).[36] Curiously, though, she does not seek to make a similar distinction between, say, Wealth as an absence of privation and luxury in the sense of overabundance and greed. Rather, her understanding of Wealth is as the polar opposite of Beggary, as monetary gain or as conspicuous over-consumption (559–561). By contrast it is worth noting that most comic utopias in the miraculous tradition focus on the satisfaction of basic demands, food and drink.[37] Moreover, Penia presents herself as guarantor of the current economic order, which raises the question: if she is not responsible for the beggars, who is? Are they accidental, irrelevant, or are they necessary for her economic orthodoxy? Penia seems conspicuously silent on this, other than disclaiming responsibility. But the logic of compulsion (526–534) that she offers sounds to me like 'the harsh discipline' of the market, or, as the current New Labour phrase would have it, 'tough choices'. Chremylus may not be so rhetorically or politically sophisticated, but he's no fool.

In addition to rhetorical hair-splitting, she also resorts to the old favourite, the mythological exemplum, whose forced nature resembles the gags about the Heraclean baths and the marital affairs of Peleus and Thetis in *Clouds* (1050–1070). But, as there, two can play that game, and in fact in the game of mythological exempla, Chremylus holds his own. In

---

[35] Bowie 1993: 288–290 compares her arguments with those of Aristotle for self-sufficiency.

[36] Bowie 1993: 288–9 is far too categorical in accepting that Penia's view, of poverty as hard-working, moderate self-sufficiency, was the standard Greek view, without further qualification. Penia's own words are *prima facie* evidence that this was precisely not the case.

[37] So Sommerstein 1984: 11, cf. Ruffell 2000.

response to his reasonable suggestion that Zeus is rich and because Zeus is wise, this shows Wealth is a Good Thing, Penia argues that the poverty of the prizes at the Olympic Games demonstrates Zeus' poverty (581–6). Chremylus gives as good as he gets by suggesting rather that this shows his concern to keep his Wealth (587–8). Penia claims that this shows Zeus acting in a slavish and greedy fashion. Although Chremylus does not immediately come back on this, it is not clear that his view is out of kilter with the general representation of the habits of individual gods elsewhere in Old Comedy. But he caps it with a final mythological/religious example of poor folk scrounging scraps from altars to Hecate, before sending Penia packing.

It is fair to say that Chremylus has little ammunition when he attempts to respond to Penia on the details of his utopian dream. But what has been less advertised is that Penia does not respond to effective points made by Chremylus when he is critiquing her position. Consider, first of all, Chremylus' savage indictment of poverty. Yes this is emotional, but that is not enough to dismiss what is an effective piece of dramatic or political rhetoric. This is a powerful statement of the privations of poverty.

> φθειρῶν δ' ἀριθμὸν καὶ κωνώπων καὶ ψυλλῶν οὐδὲ λέγω σοι
> ὑπὸ τοῦ πλήθους, αἳ βομβοῦσαι περὶ τὴν κεφαλὴν ἀνιῶσιν,
> ἐπεγείρουσαι καὶ φράζουσαι· "πεινήσεις· ἀλλ' ἐπανίστω".

> ...the number of bugs and mosquitoes and flies – impossible to count –
> which leap up and buzz around our heads,
> waking us up and insisting: "You will starve – come on, get up".
>
> *Wealth* 537–9

Chremylus follows this up by denying the hair-splitting distinction that Penia seeks to introduce: Poverty and Beggary are sisters. In response, Penia has nothing to say about serious poverty, except for introducing a topical gag about comparisons between Thrasybulus and Dionysius and sweeping on (550–4). Chremylus' attempts to present the life of poverty from the perspective of the poor man is met, finally, with the claim that he is mocking her. Critics have been happy to accept this, but clearly Penia's response is as much a rhetorical strategy as anything that Chremylus comes up with. Trying to label Chremylus' sarcasm about a life of scrimping and saving as a joke and not being serious is to ignore almost everything he has said. It is surely also curious that Penia – who is after all a figure in a comedy – should seek to label an argument as σκώπτειν πειρᾷ καὶ κωμῳδεῖν τοῦ σπουδάζειν ἀμελήσας (557). If Penia is a figure from philosophy, she is also expressing the rhetorical moves of philosophy in seeking to distinguish herself from the non-logical claims of κωμῳδία, while at the same time seeking to cover up her own.

But it would be a mistake to be suckered into this rhetoric. For, even if this is the cool argumentation that it is rational to be poor, Penia is in fact as "emotional" an arguer as is Chremylus himself. She goes on to offer a caricature of the indolent rich – in itself as "emotive" as Chremylus' description of poverty – and a utopian and nostalgic vision of the noble poor of the past. These fighting men of 561 are clearly suggestive of Aristophanes' earlier representations of *Marathonomakhoi*. It is easy enough to see why Poverty's espousing of thrift and the upstanding noble peasantry has found a receptive audience within the context of the modern Protestant work ethic and (to say nothing of other countries) the various Anglo-Saxon ideals of the solid yeomanry, citizen farmers or hardy frontiersman, but hers is an idealised vision far removed from Chremylus' version of material realities. For all that Aristophanes played around with the ideal of the farmer-hoplite-democrat in *Acharnians*, *Wasps* or *Lysistrata*, Chremylus is here confronting that ideal head-on here with miserabilism of Radiohead-like proportions.

Penia's further claim, that she will demonstrate that she leads to σωφροσύνη (563) and κοσμιότης (564), signally fails to live up to her billing. What this does reflect, though, is Penia's adherence to the Hang 'Em and Flog 'Em brigade, amongst other variants on ancient con-servatism. From the very beginning, she is shown to be a representative of Order.

> ὦ θερμὸν ἔργον κἀνόσιον καὶ παράνομον
> τολμῶντε δρᾶν ἀνθρωπαρίω κακοδαίμονε–
>
> Outrage! Infamy! Crime!
> How dare you, you little men, you scum–
>
> *Wealth* 415–6

It is the men's daring that is repeatedly stressed as upsetting her, whether that is their initial action (416, 419, 454) or their daring to gainsay her (594). Using the language of politics and punishment, the illegality of their transgressions is emphasised, as well as a relish displayed for their punishment (415, 418, 433–4, 454–5). Penia seems more concerned about Chremylus' threat to Order than his arguments. She does not respond to his claim (widely accepted outside of the Home Office) that poverty is responsible for crime, where Chremylus explicitly picks up her claim to be the party of Law and Order (565). Rather, she launches into a spiel on how poor politicians proceed to fleece the state, become rich and corrupt. If we are following the logic of this, then the injustice proceeds from the access to power, rather than from the Wealth and it is no answer (566–570). Chremylus is more than happy to agree with the Aristophanic, indeed satirical, truism that power corrupts. Penia claims ultimately to be the parent overseeing children (577–8), the gremlin on the shoulder that keeps the nose to the grindstone and the feet in line (534), explicitly a mistress (δέσποιν'), humans her slaves.[38]

If it is not clear from this that Chremylus wins the argument, it is far from obvious that he loses it either. If he has been lured into attempting to talk Penia's own language, what she has to say is deeply disturbing. Economic stability and social order are dependent upon a meek and non-questioning citizenry, where the mass are living at (at best) subsistence levels. Chremylus has articulated the problem and the need for a solution – and has one miraculously up his sleeve; Penia says, "What problem?" Both are problematic, I suggest, but both in emotional and rhetorical terms,

Chremylus is of greater substance than has often been recognised.
Comparisons with other Aristophanic contests are instructive. Chremylus is not the first (even if he is the last) Aristophanic character to blag his way out of a contest rather than winning it through the purity of his logic, nor is he the only one to insult, physically humiliate or offer violence to his interlocutor. Immediately springing to mind are Bdelycleon in *Wasps*, who tries every rhetorical stunt in the book to try to persuade his dear old dad and then resorts to outright trickery; Dicaeopolis' insulting of Lamachus; Lysistrata's handling of the Proboulos; or the confused and ambiguous

---

[38] This is disturbing in its own way as the authoritarian claims of the contemporary personification of the Laws in Plato's *Crito*.

serious of debates in *Frogs.*[39] But perhaps the most obvious parallel is the first contest in *Clouds*. The Weaker Argument deploys similar styles of arguments to Penia. The difference is that he nominally wins the argument (albeit with *ad hominem* arguments from the sexual preferences of the audience). But if the precursors to and the aftermath of the contest offer better arguments than the Stronger Argument did for the flaws in the Weaker Argument's case, the Stronger Argument himself is not easily validated. Unthinking nostalgia by itself is not enough – the Weaker Argument justifiably wins the contest – in addition to the representative of times past being somewhat conflicted in his own right. If we should learn (as well as be entertained by) their knocking lumps out of each other, then the smug hair-splitting and moral nihilism of the Weaker Argument is no more to be validated by the experience than the unthinking, uncritical certainties of the Stronger Argument. We might say, perhaps, that plagues are being wished on both their houses, but that the more resilient genes on both sides are worth investigating.

## 2.3 Politics, as Usual

If, as I have been suggesting, there is a certain amount of utopian criticism involved in the interpretation, especially the 'ironic' interpretation of the philosophical elements in the late plays, the idiosyncrasies of critics' perspectives become all the more glaring when the plays turn explicitly to politics, or rather (since the economic interests of the plays are supremely political) to the relationship between the individual citizen and the state. Interpretations of both *Ecclesiazusae* and *Wealth* depend to a large extent on the interactions of the new world order with the apparatus of the Athenian democracy. Beyond abuse of individual politicians, or politicians as a class, something already touched upon in relation to the former play, this is dramatised above all in two controversial scenes. In *Ecclesiazusae* the communalisation of property is tackled through one character who gathers together his property in line with the recent resolution of the assembly, and is confronted by a fellow-citizen who proceeds to debunk the whole scheme. In *Wealth*, there is a similar contesting of the

---

[39] The list could go on – for example, almost all the contests in *Knights* are less about shining rhetoric than about grubby political realities.

miraculous curing of Wealth by a sycophant, whose livelihood has been ruined. In this case, too, there is a pairing off of characters and positions, as the sycophant is juxtaposed with someone introduced simply as a 'good man'. These sharp dialogues do indeed pose hard questions over (respectively) the practicality and the ethics of the protagonists' schemes, but the answers that are suggested are not at all straightforward. For the ironic school (and to some extent also the literal school) of interpretation needs to acknowledge that in *Ecclesiazusae* the opposing voice questions whether the law should be, could be or generally was obeyed, while in *Wealth* the accusation is that the state and the laws are being subverted. The same voices who nod at the wise words of the second character in the former have also tended to accept the complaint of the sycophant. We could here note the different contexts in the plays and wave away consistency in (comic) interpretation. Nonetheless, this tension is, I think, interesting.

The staging of the *Ecclesiazusae* scene is as important as the arguments between the characters. Citizen A, who may or may not be Chremes or one of Blepyros' neighbours, but who at any rate seems to be the character in the previous scene who was convinced by the arguments of Praxagora,[40] assembles his possessions in order to add them to the common store, in a comic version of the Panathenaic procession. The humour of the scene derives from a number of sources – in the first place, the pun on (a literal understanding of) ἐξετάζω (729), then the shift from humans to kitchen implements and one bird (with a variety of connections between the two sides), and the shift from large to small. There is also broad scope for physical humour between Citizen A and his two slaves (867–8), bursting in and out of doors with material – in ways similar to the trial scene of *Wasps* – lining up of the parade and the tying up of the articles (785, 787). The eventual procession with the objects dangling (and no doubt jangling) on a pole (833) adds the final touch.[41]

---

[40] For the state of play on this question, see Sommerstein on 564.

[41] A slave at either end, as in Beazley 1971: 150,3, has more of a processional air than a single slave balancing a pole with objects at either end (for which see Beazley 1971: 150,4), or the example of Herakles and the Kerkopes (Carpenter 1991: 218), or having it over his shoulder, as in the opening of Frogs (this is the configuration of the 'Berlin Herakles' (Taplin 1993: 14.7)). Sommerstein puts the objects in sacks, and gives the

Of course the fictional parade (730–745) is as symbolic as anything in the genuine article. The shift to the household implements is suggestive of the way in which the *polis* has been reconfigured more as an *oikos* in line with the women's own experience.[42] As noted earlier, however, this is playing off a complex relationship between these two core elements in Athenian society.[43] The shifting of the elements of the Panathenaic procession towards the material, practical and everyday is characteristic of the materialist thrust of the play. However, the element of communal dining, which is at the heart of the new scheme, is hardly alien to the context of Athenian state festivals, including the Panathenaia.[44] At the same time, just as the Panathenaic procession had only select representatives of the people, so too are the mass of little pots kept out of Citizen A's parade.

Certainly, this is comic dislocation, but there are strong elements of continuity with the previous context, and indeed there seems to be considerable symbolic continuity. This is no simple parody. And it is against the continuities, the communal underpinnings of this scene, that the interruption by Citizen B goes. He refuses to give up his property, initially claiming that he will wait and see what everyone else is doing (750, 770–2). To Citizen A's confident report of what the popular reaction is, he presents a series of gags on the nature of the Athenians (happy to talk, not happy to trust, 771–8). He accuses the Athenians of being ever ready to change their minds (a thread in Aristophanes going back to *Acharnians*, and the point of Praxagora's earlier speech), and there are a catalogue of examples– collective, individual, even divine. This is strong stuff. The denial of altruism goes to the heart of both the critique implicit in the actions of the women and the structures of the new state. As far as the character of the Athenians – no, let us say the human race – it seems that

---

'tripods' (787) to the second slave to carry, but this seems unnecessarily complicating, and less funny. Slater 2002: 221 seems to miss the carrying-pole.

[42] See Foley 1982, Bowie 1993: 262–4.

[43] Bowie 1993 suggests that the festive aspect of the Panathenaia points to success, but claims that "Aristophanes' earlier plays and the fact that the procession is composed of household goods suggest something different". I suggest rather that the household nature of the goods is not decisive by itself, and so his ironic reading of this scene is largely for the sake of consistency with his readings of the other plays, which is a problematic strategy.

[44] See the study of Schmitt-Pantel 1992.

not only is Citizen A fully in agreement with Citizen B, but that the audience are being cued in to laugh at their agreement.

If this were all, it would look black for progressive (or at least optimistic) readings of the *Ecclesiazusae*. Certainly critics have tended to accept as self-evident the proposition that Citizen B is confronting Citizen A with unalterable facts of human nature, and with the triumph of globalized, corporate capitalism in the 1980s and 1990s, who could argue? The self-evident lesson of the entire scene is that "a state cannot operate on the same terms of shared interest and informal negotiations as the household", as Helene Foley puts it (1982: 16).

But it is not all. In addition to Citizen B's pessimistic reading of the character of the Athenians (which looks like being borne out by the arguments), we find a direct challenge to the laws:

– τὶ δ᾽; οὐχὶ πειθαρχεῖν με τοῖς νόμοισι δεῖ;
– ποίοισιν, ὦ δύστηνε;
–                              τοῖς δεδογμένοις.
– δεδογμένοισιν; ὡς ἀνόητος ἦσθ᾽ ἄρα.

– What? Shouldn't I obey the laws?
– What ones are they, you poor sod?
– The ones that have been agreed at the assembly.
– The ones that have been agreed? Dear me, you're totally clueless.

*Eccl.* 762–4

This locates us in the heady territory of whether citizens have a duty to obey the law (*Antigone, Crito*), perhaps also of how 'democratic' democracy really is. δεδογμένοισιν points equally to the technical language of Athenian decision-making and to the debates around conventional νόμος in late Fifth-Century thought.[45] With the explicit contrast with the Athenians' rather divergent πάτριον νόμον (778), the suggestion that law is an arbitrary convention (and check on human nature) comes to the fore. In this context, it is not simply a matter of questioning altruism, solidarity, mutual aid or (my own favourite) fluffy con-sensualism, but of questioning any social contract at all. That this was a live political and philosophical issue, stemming from the upheavals in the

---

[45] See Ober 1999, Rothwell 1990: 62.

aftermath of the Peloponnesian War, is clear enough both from legislation (against breach of the constitution), the implication of leading intellectuals and their associates, and Plato's response in *Apology* and *Crito*. That the actions of the Thirty would have led to Citizen B's rhetorical pose being dismissed out of hand is harder to say, not least given the legally dubious actions of Aristophanic protagonists from Dicaeopolis through to Praxagora.

However it is a pose. If there are choices to be made over obedience to the law, then the rest of Athens appears to make it. The entrance of the Herald interrupts this chain of thought by announcing that the communal feast is ready. The clear implication that (enough) property had been collected for the new state to become viable. Citizen B equally clearly takes it as such and smoothly changes gear. No longer is the question over whether the citizens will obey the laws and persuading Citizen A of the fact, but rather it turns to what he can get out of himself. The tables are turned. Just as earlier he posed a barrage of 'what if' questions to his neighbour about the consequences of being the sole loyal citizen, now, in a passage that directly mirrors the earlier, the neighbour demands to know how he will blag his way into the feast. A series of increasingly impractical propositions are suggested by Citizen B, culminating in theft of the most blatant kind, and it seems as if he has nowhere to turn.

It is fascinating, though, to see how Citizen B is handled by critics. As a shorthand, he is labelled 'The Skeptic' (Ober) or 'The Dissident' (Sommerstein), suggesting perhaps a Protagoras or a Sakharov. In reality, he is neither the one nor the other. His is not a position of moral or philosophical principle so much as personal profit.[46] He is the embodiment of the greed and self-interest that has been satirized throughout the play. For that reason, it is also too simplistic to rule him out as a 'scofflaw' (Slater): rather he (together with the issues he raises) plugs into the broader network of thematically connected displays of political and economic self-interest. It has been noted that in his selfishness, Citizen B mirrors some Aristophanic protagonists – certainly true of Strepsiades, but the more interesting comparison is with Dicaeopolis, in *Acharnians*. Here we have

---

[46] I find it difficult to see the rat-a-tat-tat questions of a mimicking of the Socratic elenchus (Ober). Rather it is comic q-and-a, along the lines of *Lys.* 157–164, but setting up a comic reversal.

to make a very sharp distinction between legality and morality.[47] For Dicaeopolis (or so he claims), his personal peace is a moral matter, but certainly of questionable legality. Citizen B disdains any ethics beyond crude self-interest. The crucial distinction, as with all Aristophanic characters, is the moral background to their decisions, and here Citizen B is more akin to the undeserving people wanting a share (such as Lamachus). He is refusing to give a share and then (almost in the next breath) selfishly trying to grab a share.

But there is one more anxiety for the irony-prone. As Citizen A moves off, his procession in tow, Citizen B is left to conclude the scene alone.

> νὴ τὸν Δία δεῖ γοῦν μηχανήματός τινος,
> ὅπως τὰ μὲν ὄντα χρήμαθ' ἔξω, τοῖσδέ τε
> τῶν ματτομένων κοινῇ μεθέξω πως ἐγώ.
> ὀρθῶς, ἔμοιγε φαίνεται· βαδιστέον
> ὁμόσ' ἐστὶ δειπνήσοντα κοὐ μελλητέον.

> By Zeus, then, I need some scheme
> to make sure I keep my possessions, and that I
> can somehow grab a share of what's being cooked up for them all together.
> Right, it's clear to me anyway: I need to go
> as quick as possible to get my dinner and not hang about.
>
> *Eccl.* 872–4

Recent commentators have worried about the last word going to Citizen B unchallenged. But more than that, it is the construction put upon his words that has become significant. Between 874 and 875, they have assumed that Citizen B comes up with some killer plan which will allow him to grab a share at no cost to him, thus proving if not his entire contention, then at least that there are operational holes in the scheme, and (almost inevitably) showing that communism is a dead duck. However, is there really anything to support this edifice erected upon a supposed pause? It is suggested that ὀρθῶς points to something that he has been thinking of, but if so, the obvious thought is his immediately prior statement that he must get some food. The ὀρθῶς is then approving this idea and leading to the conclusion that he needs to go to the banquet as quickly as possible. That's it. After

---

[47] *Contra* Slater 2002, for whom the illegality of Citizen B is a mark of immorality.

we have seen all his practical suggestions shot down by Citizen A, all we are left with is the bare idea, which is not looking terribly promising, that he needs to get some food without contributing somehow.[48]

So, although Citizen B has the final words, they hardly undermine the scheme of Praxagora as it is unfolding within the fictional world of the play. Although critics have worried that they go unanswered, this is not really a problem, as there is nothing further to answer that we have not seen already. Indeed, it would be more than a little unfair to criticise the communist fellow travellers for failing to answer something that is never actually articulated (Hayekian economics? a sharp stick?). Given the movement of this scene, as outlined above, the interaction with Citizen B does not so much offer an ironic undercurrent as multiple satirical critiques - of Athenian politics (which everyone can agree on), of unscrupulous use of rhetorical and/or philosophical moves for unscrupulous and selfish ends, and ultimately of pursuit of self-interest despite all evidence to the contrary. In a sense, it doesn't really matter whether we imagine that there are more people like Citizen B lurking in the background – the important thing is the juxtaposition of the selfish and the altruistic and communal, not suggesting that the mad, implausible and possibly (for an Athenian male) quite tasteless proposal is the answer to all their problems (though you never know) but that Citizen B and people like him may be a significant cause of those problems.

However, if the lack of answer given to Citizen B is seen as a problem by some, in *Wealth*, the anxieties over another critic in the political sphere are because he is all-too-emphatically answered, in the inimical fashion of the pro-redistribution crowd in that play – the sophisticated dialectic of a good kicking. And who is the unfortunate victim? A sycophant. Again, there is an interesting parallel with the *Acharnians*, where we get to see a sycophant in action, and Dicaeopolis retaliating by packing him up and bartering him to the Theban. Here, though, the sycophant is given rather more time and space to justify himself. Given the different sort of utopia explored in this play (compared with *Ecclesiazusae* or, for that matter, *Acharnians*), the nature of the objections are going to be different too, but

---

[48] Ussher *ad loc.* points to Plato, *Protagoras* 359e7–360a2, where Socrates acknowledges agreement to his point and moves on to draw the conclusion; but this does not help us pinpoint a lost brainwave.

they are a fascinating reversal of the objections of Citizen B. Whereas Citizen B argued against any illegality, the sycophant here argues that he is, in effect, the embodiment of the law – and more than that of the entire Athenian democracy. For some critics, the removal of this troublesome litigant serves to show that the new society is based on injustice and the overturning of democratic structures (so Olson 1990).

Again we need to look at the movement of the scene. Just as a clue, the sycophant is juxtaposed with an anonymous character whose major attribute is that he is a Good Man τῶν χρηστῶν τις (826), who was latterly (by extension) poor. Under the new regime of cured Wealth, the Good Man has gained riches and was in the process of dedicating his worn-out cloak to the god. The sycophant comes in wailing in over-the-top fashion (note the extent to which he is wretched at 850–3), and this prompts much speculation as to what has happened to him. The conclusion is that he must be bad currency, τοῦ πονηροῦ κόμματος (862). The coinage metaphor becomes something of a running joke (see also 957), and with its implication of crooked Wealth is clearly thematically related to the issue of Wealth in the play. Likewise, the ongoing suggestion that he is a 'ned, housebreaker ... and thief'[49] is hardly a neutral introduction. As it becomes clear (or more explicit) who he is, Cario and the Good Man reflect on how his fall from Wealth is a deserved fate.

For his own part, the sycophant does nothing to make himself a more attractive figure. He sprays around threats like confetti. First he threatens to blind (judicially) Wealth again, then he is convinced (with no evidence whatsoever) that Cario (or his master) or the Good Man or Wealth have stolen his money and suggests reprisals. Then he accuses Cario and the Good Man of treating him with hybris because they are not respecting his authority. Both his violence and his arrogance are clearly on display. And then he declares himself to be φιλόπολις and, indeed, χρηστός (900). In the context of Aristophanic comedy, those are fighting words; in the context of *Wealth* he is directly contesting the already-established credentials of his credentials, whose fate, moreover, meshes with the ethico-ontological nature of the world of cured Ploutos. But, to give the sycophant his due,

---

[49] As graciously formulated by ex-MSP Kenny Gibson, SECC, May 2, 2003, referring to the Scottish Socialist Party. See *Wealth* 869, 909, 939.

what does he do to earn these epithets? Does he do anything useful – as farmer, merchant or craftsman? Does he actually do anything? Apparently not, but nonetheless the sycophant in typically over-the-top fashion claims that he has control of all the city's affairs, public and private (907–8). But all he does is want, βούλομαι. This apparent paradox sets up a punchline that may or may not be seen coming (908). Because 'anyone who wants' can initiate prosecutions, the sycophant claims to have taken the 'wanting' as a role, trade or way of life. This is (depending on how you look on it) either verbal deceit by the character or a good verbal play by the poet, but this points to the core issue. Prosecutions are not the same thing as a trade, except insofar as one earns a living off them – i.e. they are anything from self-interested to overtly malicious. Moreover, prosecutions are not the exclusive competence of sycophants. Indeed, for all the claims of the sycophant to uphold the law and ensure guilty men are punished, the counter-argument that that is the responsibility of jurors is not really denied.[50]

So when the sycophant is asked whether interfering, πολυπραγμονεῖν, is the same as public service, εὐεργετεῖν (913), this goes to the heart of the matter. It is far from clear that the sycophant is acting in the spirit of the ὁ βουλόμενος principle. Rather he goes well beyond the idea of a democracy based on active citizenship, when he claims that he – and people like him – are responsible for all the city's affairs, public or private. The language is reminiscent of that used of prominent populist politicians, not individual responsibility.[51] The arbitrary nature of the sycophant's position is reinforced by the running joke on 'whoever wants', as it is suggested he might just as easily 'want' to give it up (921); or as he makes the mistake of asking ὁ βουλόμενος to have a go at him – with disastrous results.

Nor, on the other side, is it clear that the quiet life, offered as an alternative, is defined much beyond not-acting-like-a-sycophant. The sycophant's response, that it is the "life of a sheep" is provocative, but seriously undermined by his qualification, "if there's no obvious occupation for your life", εἰ μὴ φανεῖται διατριβή τις τῷ βίῳ (922–3).

---

[50] The division of lines between Cario and the Good Man are not absolutely clear in much of this scene, but that's

largely because they are coming at the question from a similar perspective.

[51] Note προστάτην (920) and ἐπιμελητὴς (907).

Although he is being offered a rest from his own profession, it is quite clear from the rest of the scene that a quiet life might be entirely compatible with a range of activities or crafts (which certainly count as a διατριβή). Whatever the superficial similarities, we are, here, far from a simple inversion of the language of Thucydides' Funeral Speech.

So, it is possible to contest the sycophant's claims on the point of principle, and this indeed is done directly and also indirectly through implication and metaphor. On the other, we can see that, whatever the claim, the sycophant's actions are presented as being motivated by (again) greed and self-interest, coupled with a vicious and arrogant streak. It's that hyperbolic arrogance that leads the sycophant to claim that he is the democracy. And that violent element, with the logic of comic reversal, makes him a particularly good target for stage violence. Again, we are left with the clear indication that it is not simply a matter of legality = morality, or even that legality = democracy. Rather, the operation of those laws is up for negotiation, as is the morality behind the use of those laws. If the curing of Wealth is in any number of senses stepping outside of political norms and systems, the interesting question becomes: is it in the spirit of the political system? Or, what is or what should be the spirit of the political system and why has it been corrupted?

These two scenes in *Ecclesiazusae* and *Wealth*, then, come at the question of laws, politics and morals from different directions. For ironic readings of the plays, it needs to be shown clearly why the illegality of the one is approved (or acknowledged as 'realistic') and the claims of the other of legal propriety, or indeed of being constitutionally essential, are accepted. As I hope to have shown, the movement of the scenes questions the claims of both, either that self-interested actions are inevitable or that self-appointed, self-interested prosecutors are the quintessence of the state. They share at root the foregrounding of fickleness, injustice, self-interest and the lure of money within the Athenian political system, and in their opponents a naive hope in trust and altruism. The miraculous cure has its miraculously redistributive effects, but also in the case of the *Ecclesiazusae* the citizens also all dine (1130–3), which suggests (even if it doesn't prove) that Blepyros' trust in his neighbours is well-founded, the joke at 1177–8 notwithstanding. This is not to suggest that Aristophanes is advocating either communism or finding a convenient god to sort things out. Rather, we have a critique of the status quo, but it also raises the question of what kind of social or economic order is wanted. And, well, if it could work like this, wouldn't it be good?

## 3 Conclusion: Whose Irony Is It Anyway?

It seems clear that the reasons why *Ecclesiazusae* and *Wealth* have proved so problematic to critics is that they venture into explicit political and economic territory in ways unmatched by the other extant plays, even by the outrageous possibilities of an *Acharnians* or a *Peace*. As I have suggested, care is taken to ramp up the plausibility of the schemes of the protagonists – these are in no sense 'safe' dramas – and it seems to be this anxiety that has prompted critics to force them into an ironic strait-jacket, to a greater or lesser extent. As I have suggested, ironic interpretations are problematic in that they make even more assumptions than ostensibly 'straightforward' interpretations, but in fact both sides of that debate are reducing the complexity of what is actually happening on stage.

But there is perhaps a further reason why the plays invite ironic readings. With both plays, the role of the protagonist is seriously diminished, beyond the establishment of the new world orders. This is not only with Praxagora (where there are similarities with *Lysistrata* that suggest that this is to some extent determined by gender politics) but also Chremylus in *Wealth*. And as well as sheer stage presence, the names of the protagonists are far less directional than in many of the earlier plays. Instead the plays are dominated with parts that are anonymous or blandly named, with little stage time, mostly male, but also some female. Some of these are related to the 'intruders' of the earlier plays, but they are much more provocative – not (or not only) wanting a slice of the action, but exemplifying different reactions in the wider population, or making objections to their new circumstances. Without the somewhat stifling effect of the protagonist, the field of play becomes much wider, and the projections of critics much more open.

We can go further. For *Ecclesiazusae*, at least, there is metatheatrical play with the audience, at least until the agon, where Praxagora is setting out her scheme to her husband. This fits clearly with the corporate critiques of the Athenians *en masse* throughout the rehearsals for the assembly.[52] With the translation to the individual Panathenaia and the debate over individual response, we move away from the confrontation of the mass audience to individual reflection, choice and reactions by the anonymous characters. This interest in the individual response, in the audience as in the fictional world, is arguably enacted in the structure of the *Ecclesiazusae*. The interest in and acknowledgement of the individual Athenian's decisions, responsibilities and response is what marks out the late plays from the earlier. Combined with the provocative content, this new focus on the individual everyman and everywoman is inviting the question, "Well, what would you do?"

From this perspective, the old debate between the ironists and the non-ironists is on both sides an exercise in utopian criticism – on the one side an attempt to maintain a smooth veneer of logic and coherence within a comic context; on the other an attempt to negate the positive side of the dialectic in order to create an equally uniform logic of critique. Neither, I suggest, is adequate to the true problems that confront us – which are the nature of comic rhetoric and the nature of audience response. Indeed, if faith in utopias has been sorely tried over the past century, I would suggest that an unquestioning faith in irony is not adequate either (and I include in that the work of Slavoj Žižek – but that's another paper entirely). As with the early Alan Sommerstein, I do want to resurrect the principle of hope and I do want to suggest that the texts of Aristophanes' late plays make efforts to render this plausible. But as the more recent Alan Sommerstein has conceded, we cannot ignore the dialogic aspects of the plays either. Both ironic and non-ironic are in a sense hard-coded in *Ecclesiazusae* and *Wealth*. What we can see in this case, as with most radical conceptual humour, this sets up a clash of plausibilities which critique each other and which provide ample ammunition for spectators to think with. And, to an extent not matched by the earlier plays, these late comedies are prepared to explore and countenance the nature of individual response.

But that's not to say that there are not directions and structures which are pointing audience responses in certain directions. I have suggested that much of the full-blown ironic interpretations rely on double standards or

---

[52] For recent analysis, see Slater 2002, although it will be clear that I disagree with his analysis of the metatheatricality as introducing a distancing frame of implausibility.

special pleading, but it is a testament to the openness of the late plays that critics have been able to make those moves. What we can say above all is that these plays are critiquing a logic of selfishness and self-interest, and exploring instead notions of trust, altruism and solidarity, not with a concrete program for revolutionary change but as progressive thought-experiments. In a sense, then, these late plays are posing the same complex problem as that old anti-globalisation slogan – "Let's replace capitalism with something nicer" – both positively exploring the practical and ethical means that this would require and at the same time a critique of existing material realities and ideological contexts. This is not to turn Aristophanes into a dry, philosophical text. On the contrary, it is precisely because it is comic discourse that it can exploit such multiple strands in such a condensed way. All this is potentially explosive material – whether it detonates or not is up to the audience.[53]

[53] The distant roots of this paper lie in an Oxford seminar on *Wealth* led by Dr. P. A. Bulloch and Professor P. J. Parsons. The discussion on those occasions informs my treatment throughout, although both the argument and its misconceptions are entirely my own. I'd also like to thank Chloe Stewart, Gideon Nisbet and Catherine Steel for their characteristic help, and John Rich for inviting me in the first place. I realized to my alarm after submitting the title that my contrived allusion to Alanis Morissette's song, 'Ironic' (track 1 on *Jagged Little Pill* [Maverick, 1995}) continues the long tradition of Ruffell misquotes.

# On first looking into Kratinos'
## *Dionysalexandros*[1]

## *Ian Storey*

### (Trent University, Ontario)

Unlike tragedy, where we have complete dramas by at least three poets spanning seventy years, for the study of Old Comedy we have complete plays by one poet only, Aristophanes, whose eleven extant comedies span just under forty years (career: 427–*c*.385). For certain of the lost tragedies and satyr-plays, ancient *testimonia*, substantial preserved fragments and modern papyrus discoveries have combined to provide a great deal of information about both plot and treatment, but there are very few comedies about whose plot-line and characters we can speak with any confidence. If we had more substantial remains of the other poets of Old Comedy (ideally a complete play), we could better place Aristophanes in context and provide answers to certain critical questions. Was Aristophanes' topical/political comedy, laced with personal jokes, sophisticated parody, and low humour the norm or the exception in the late fifth century? What other sorts of comedy were being produced and winning prizes? Did a major change come over comedy in the 420s with the advent of the next generation of comedians (Aristophanes, Eupolis, Phrynichos, and Platon)? What happened with the 'next generation' of comic poets who lead us into 'Middle Comedy'?

In fact, apart from the original version of *Clouds* (423–D), the only comedies that we can 'restore' to any great degree are: Eupolis' *Marikas* (421–L), thanks to a reasonable number of traditional fragments and portions of a papyrus commentary (fr. 192); Eupolis' *Demoi* (417?), again owing to considerable fragments, plus 120 lines on three papyrus leaves

---

[1] In the interest of consistency and to avoid switching back and forth between 'Paris' and 'Alexandros', I will refer to him as 'Alexandros', the name that appears as part of the title.

published in 1911 (fr. 99), and the depiction of a scene from the comedy on a Paestan vase from the 4th century; and Kratinos' brilliantly meta-theatrical *Pytine* (423–D), in which the poet becomes his own chief character. But in all these cases considerable doubt remains over the plot-line and eventual comic conclusion. Then there is the subject of my paper, Kratinos' *Dionysalexandros*, arguably the play of Old Comedy about which we are best informed apart from those of Aristophanes. Here we actually do know how the comedy unfolded, developed, and concluded, with an intriguing hint of a topical sub-text.

Our detailed knowledge of this comedy is due not to the fragments preserved in the literary tradition, which are not that many or that extensive (frr. 39–51, about sixteen lines) or from a papyrus discovery of a substantial new text, but from the publication over a century ago of *POxy.* 663 (2nd/3rd c. AD), most of a summary of the comedy's plot (hypothesis), very likely originating from the Alexandrian period. My purpose in this paper honouring Alan Sommerstein and his invaluable series of commentaries on Aristophanes' extant plays is to provide some first thoughts in re-assessing what we can say about this lost comedy, a century or so after the appearance of *POxy.* 663.

## *POxy 663*[2]

The text of the hypothesis survives in two columns, with a three-line heading at the top of the right-hand column (ΔIONYC[/H/KPAT[) and some text missing at the start of the left-hand column. It is not clear how much has been lost before we can pick up the narrative – I shall argue below that only an early scene (or series of scenes) has been lost. Abbreviations are used frequently in the text, e.g. μτδεται in line 20 for μετὰ δὲ ταῦτα, and in a few places (see below) there is doubt about the actual text or its meaning – these are indicated in italics below in my translation. But on the whole the plot of Kratinos' comedy is reasonably easy to follow.

---

[2] The original publication is that of Grenfell and Hunt (1904). Recent presentations of the text are: Luppe (1966: 169–70); Austin (1973) nr. 70, pp. 35–7; K.-A. IV (1983: 140–1); Rosen (1988: 50–1).

Luppe (1966: between 178–9) presents a useful photograph of the papyrus.

. . . judgement Hermes [5] leaves, while they say some things to the spectators *concerning the poets* [or *concerning the begetting of sons*] and joke and make fun of Dionysos when he appears [10]. When *[the goddesses and Hermes]* enter and <promise> him <gifts>, from Hera unshaken tyranny, from Athena [15] courage [or 'success'] in war, and from Aphrodite to make him very beautiful and attractive, he judges her [Aphrodite] to be the winner. After this he sails [20] to Sparta, takes Helen, and returns to Ida. A little while later he hears that the Greeks are ravaging the countryside [25] *and <looking for>* Alexandros. Very quickly he hides Helen in a basket [30] and turns himself into a ram to await developments. <The real> Alexandros enters and detecting both of them [35] orders them to be led to the ships, intending to hand them over to the Greeks. When Helen refuses, he takes pity on her and retains possession of her, to keep her as his wife. Dionysos he dispatches to be handed over [40]. The satyrs go along with him, maintaining that they will not betray him. In this play Perikles [45] is very convincingly made fun of by innuendo (δι' ἐμφάσεως) for having brought the war on the Athenians.

The publication of the hypothesis confirmed the suspicion of Grauert (1828), followed by Kock (1880: 23), that the comedy was a mythological burlesque in which Dionysos replaced Alexandros for the famous judgement with predictably comic results. Meineke (1839: 1.56–7), thinking that 'Alexandros' should refer to Alexander the Great, attributed the play to the younger Kratinos and saw the comedy as turning on Alexander's recreation of the travels of Dionysos to the East with the pomp of a Dionysiac procession.

Three places in the hypothesis present significant problems of text and interpretation. The first (lines 7–9) is a well-worn controversy. The first and third lines are clear, 'to the spectators … they say'. The text of the second (line 8) suffers from abbreviation, but appears to read: τιναπυωνποιη.This was expanded by the initial editors (Grenfell & Hunt 1904: 72) to π(ερὶ) ὑῶν ποιή(cεωc), which should at first sight mean something like 'about the begetting of pigs', but was interpreted by Rutherford (1904) as 'concerning the begetting of sons', and as referring to Perikles' legitimation of his son by Aspasia after the death of his other sons in the plague (Plutarch, *Perikles* 37), Rutherford assuming a date in 429 (see below) and that Perikles played a major role beneath the surface of the entire comedy. But Körte (1904: 495), expanding and emending the text to π(ερὶ) τῶν ποιη(τῶν), 'concerning the poets', saw the chorus' address to the spectators as a sort of parabatic interruption, and cited the very similar language in *Hypothesis III Peace* (lines 20–1, Olson) referring to the parabasis of that comedy, 'and the chorus talks to the spectators (πρὸς τοῖς θεαταῖς διαλέγεται) about the poet's craft (περὶ τῆς τοῦ ποιητοῦ τέχνης) and certain other things'.[3] Handley (1982) retained the reading, 'on the begetting of sons', bringing in *POxy*. 2806, a fragment on the 'instant family', which he attributed *Dionysalexandros*, and seeing no reference at all to the younger Perikles. As Luppe (1988) has offered a persuasive defence of Körte's reading, I am content to leave line 8 as 'concerning the poets', especially in light of the close parallel in language with the hypothesis of *Peace*.

At lines 12–19 we get a summary of the gifts offered as bribes to Alexandros, as presented comically by Kratinos.[4] Blass (1906: 486) observed that something seems to be missing after ὁ δ(ὲ) πα/ραγενομένων and before the actual description of the enticements of the goddesses, offering παραγενομένων <τῶν ἐριζομένων θεῶν καὶ προτεινομένων>, 'when the contesting goddesses appear and offer him'. Edmonds (1957: 32), accepted by Luppe (1966: 174), suggested something along the lines of τῶν θεῶν μεθ' Ἑρμ(οῦ) καὶ διδομένων, διδόναι being the operative verb in the description of the goddesses' promises at Euripides, *Trojan Women* 925, 930 and again at Isokrates 10.41. More problematic is the promise of Aphrodite, 'to make him very attractive and desirable', since other accounts give Aphrodite's enticement as marriage with Helen – as at *Trojan Women* 929–31, 'Aphrodite admiring my beauty promised me to him, if she should win the prize for beauty' and Isokrates 10.41, 'Aphrodite <promising> marriage with Helen'. Luppe (1966: 179) postulated a lacuna after Ἀφροδί(της) suggesting *exempli gratia*,

---

[3] Grenfell and Hunt (1904: 72) cite Blass's suggestion ὑπὲρ τοῦ ποιητοῦ 'which makes good sense but is rather a drastic change'. Schwarze (1971: 23 n. 39) gives further examples of the manner in which Aristophanic hypotheses refer to the chorus speaking for the poet in a parabasis.

[4] In all likelihood the goddesses did not speak directly to Dionysos-Alexandros – not enough actors available – but Hermes will have presented their proposed bribes on their behalf, just as he speaks for Peace at *Peace* 657–728. See Norwood (1931: 123); Heath (1990: 145).

ὑπισχνουμένης αὐτῷ τὴν Ἑλένην τὴν Λάκαιναν καλλίστην οὖσαν πασῶν τῶν γυναικῶν διὰ τὸ ('Aphrodite promising him Helen of Sparta, the fairest of all women, because of his being very attractive and desirable'). Ebert (1978: 179–81) emended the text to produce τῆς δ' Ἀφροδί(της) καλλιστό(ν) τε κ(αὶ) ἐπεραστότ(ατον) γάμον ὑπάρχειν ('from Aphrodite to give <him> the most beautiful and attractive marriage [bride]'). Luppe (1980) changed the text to make the promise of Helen most explicit, proposing τῆς δ' Ἀφροδί(της) <τὴν> καλλίστη(ν) τε κ(αὶ) ἐπεραστοτ(άτην) αὐτῷ ὑπάρχειν ('from Aphrodite to give him the most beautiful and desirable woman'). Flickinger's early and attractive proposal (1910: 9 n. 1) is to accept the dative αὐτῷ but keep the neuters <τὸ> κάλλιστόν τε καὶ ἐπέραστον as an indefinite 'what was most beautiful and attractive'.[5]

Rosen (1988: 52 n. 49) defends the received text, taking it to refer to Perikles' lack of physical beauty, and cites a suggestion by Koenen, 'before Pericles could expect to win Aspasia's (= Helen's) favor, his own physique would have to be transformed'. As I will argue below that Perikles does not lurk consistently beneath the comic figure of Dionysos, the received text can be defended if we regard Aphrodite's promise of beauty and attractiveness as addressed to a hedonistic and self-indulgent Dionysos, especially one wearing the ugly mask and costume of the comic actor.[6]

The final textual problem is less serious but does have some significance for the plot of the comedy. In lines 23–5 + 29 (lines 26–8 comprising the title of the head of the second column) we have 'Dionysos hears (hearing?) that the Greeks πυρ[...]εῖν the country ... Alexandros'. It is difficult to see what verb other than πυρπολεῖν could fit in the text of lines 24–5, but what follows with Alexandros as its object is less clear. Earlier critics, expanding ἀκου to ἀκούσας and relying on a tentative φ in the papyrus, needed a main verb with Dionysos as subject and Alexandros as object – hence φεύγει or φοβεῖται.[7] But if Alexandros has yet to appear

---

[5] It might be worth observing that a neuter is used for the object of love at Sappho fr. 16.4, a poem that also has to do with Helen.

[6] In the comedy Hermes may have reported Aphrodite's offer as 'she promises to make you so beautiful and attractive <that no woman can resist you>'. See Norwood (1931: 119).

[7] Grenfell and Hunt (1904: 72) – φεύγει πρὸς; Wilamowitz (ap. Luppe 1966: 180) φοβεῖται.

in the comedy, any relationship between him and Dionysos seems unlikely. Luppe (1966: 180–1) more plausibly expanded to ἀκούει and sought a second infinitive at the end of line 25 with the Greeks as subject, διώκειν or ζητεῖν. As far as the Greeks (and also Helen, one presumes) are concerned, the abductor is Alexandros of Troy, not a disguised Dionysos.

## *Structural implications*

Whether we read 'about the poets' or 'about the begetting of sons', the words in line 7 'to the spectators' make it clear that at this point in the comedy the chorus broke the dramatic illusion and addressed the audience – not that maintaining the illusion was ever a high priority of an Old Comic poet. In the extant plays of Aristophanes the chorus's address 'to the spectators' usually occurs in a parabasis, both the first parabasis (as in the parabasis proper in the comedies of the 420s – in particular see *Peace* 732–3, ἡμεῖς δ' αὖ τοῖσι θεαταῖς / ἣν ἔχομεν ὁδὸν λόγων εἴπωμεν – 'let us again speak to the spectators our path of words') and also in the second parabasis, although at *Clouds* 1115 and *Birds* 1102 the address is to the judges rather than the spectators. Earlier critics thus assumed that this part of the hypothesis was referring to a parabasis,[8] and since parabases in Aristophanes occur in the mid-part of the comedy (the earliest begins at line 498 of *Knights*), a fair bit of dramatic action was lost in the missing part of the hypothesis.

Croiset (1904), for example, thought that Hermes arrived with the goddesses in tow, who were appalled at the conditions in which a shepherd would live. Here, he thought, belonged three of the traditional fragments:

> and in there are the shearing-knives, with which
> we shear the sheep, and the shepherds (fr. 39),
>
> do you want door-posts and decorated porches ?(fr. 42),
>
> no, but to walk on fresh cow-patties and sheep dung (fr. 43).

Not finding Alexandros at home, Hermes was forced to seek a substitute in Dionysos. Thieme (1908: 7–21) argued that even more took place here. As early vases show a reluctant or even a fleeing Alexandros and later writers

---

[8] As at Blass (1906), Luppe (1966: 172), Schwarze (1971: 9–11), Rosen (1988: 58).

mention the terror felt by Alexandros when confronted with the prospect of judging these deities,[9] he suggested that such a scene would have appeared in the early part of the play.[10] Schwarze (1971: 9–11), accepting Wilamowitz's (1904) φοβεῖται in line 25, assumed that Dionysos' fear of Alexandros stemmed from their encounter earlier in the comedy. But the events as described in the hypothesis after line 9 seem enough to fill a play, and there need not be as much missing as these critics suggest. Luppe (1966: 172) argued that the participle παραγενόμενος, used twice in the hypothesis (12–13 of the goddesses and 33–4 of Alexandros), refers to the *first* appearance of a character in the drama. If this is correct, then neither the goddesses nor Alexandros appeared in the first scene(s) of the comedy. If παραφανέντα, used of Dionysos in line 10, is used in a deliberate distinction with παραγενόμενος,[11] then Dionysos *was* a character in the early part of the play, and what occasions the jeering and laughter of the satyrs is his re-appearance in vastly changed apparel, that of a mountain shepherd.

Thus we need not assume a scene or scenes of any great length before the hypothesis picks up. Perhaps we may envisage an entry of a harried and distressed Hermes, seeking an absent Alexandros for the judgement of beauty. Lucian's *Judgement* begins with Zeus' command to Hermes regarding the judgement; Kratinos may have begun his comedy with Hermes relating his instructions and his present dilemma. He may have encountered someone to whom he imparts his problem, or perhaps just delivers an exasperated soliloquy to the spectators. The entry of Dionysos will have provided Hermes with a way out of his predicament, or just possibly the substitution was related by Hermes – but there is good humour to be had from the contrast between the traditional luxury-loving Dionysos and his subsequent appearance as Alexandros. Fr. 40 of the

---

[9] E.g. a tripod *kothon* by the C Painter (Paris, Louvre CA 616) or a neck amphora by Lydos (Florence 70995); see Lucian *Judgement* 7 for Alexandros' fear in the literary tradition.

[10] See also Perdrizet (1905).

[11] Norwood (1931: 120) infers from παραφανέντα that Dionysos enters in a casual or jaunty fashion.

comedy presents an exchange between two characters, one of whom must be Hermes:[12]

> A. Now what was he wearing? Tell me this.
> B. A *thyrsos*, saffron robe [*krokotos*], quite elaborate, and a drinking-cup.

This suggests strongly that Dionysos' physical appearance was a major theme in the comedy.

Whether the chorus is talking 'about the poets' or 'about the creating of sons', it is clear that this was an extradramatic address 'to the spectators'. If there was only a scene or two missing at the start, then this chorus was talking 'to the spectators' much earlier than in an Aristophanic comedy, perhaps in what we call the parodos as opposed to the parabasis. Earlier critics seemed wedded to the notions that an address 'to the spectators' belongs in a parabasis and that a parabasis belongs well into the action of a comedy. But the hypothesis to *Dionysalexandros* suggests that in this comedy the chorus addressed the spectators during its formal entry on stage. Here it is worth comparing the parodos of *Frogs*, where the chorus addresses the spectators in anapests (354–71), the usual metre of parabasis proper, and when we get to the actual parabasis (674–737), there are no anapests. Aristophanes, it seems, has transferred the parabasis proper to the parodos.

Critics of Old Comedy have tended to assume that other comic poets will have followed the structural model and comic practice of Aristophanes. But I have argued (Storey 2003: 128) that fr. 99 of Eupolis' *Demoi*, universally regarded as part of a parabasis, might in fact be part of the parodos of that comedy, while fr. 205 of *Marikas*, two anapaestic lines 'at the beginning of the play', encourages the spectators directly to 'wake up and wash today's poetic nonsense from their eyes'. Aristophanes does address his audience 'concerning the poets' early in his comedies, but usually through his actors in the prologue (as at *Wasps* 54–66); in

---

[12] If Hermes is A, then he has been alerted to the presence of someone who might be Alexandros or fill in for him; B in that case could be the chorus or someone whom Hermes encounters in the opening scenes. If Hermes is B, then he could be explaining (to the chorus as A?) whom he has enlisted to his cause. See Norwood (1931: 120).

Kratinos, it appears, the chorus could appeal to the spectators during their entry-song.[13]

## The Date of the Comedy

Most critics begin with the statement at the end of the hypothesis, 'in the play Perikles is made fun of very convincingly through innuendo for having brought the war upon the Athenians', and conclude that 'the war' must be the Peloponnesian War that broke out in 431.[14] Since Perikles was dead by the autumn of 429, available years for *Dionysalexandros* would seem to be 430 or 429, with priority given to the former. The critics also call attention to Hermippos fr. 47, probably from his *Moirai*, in which Perikles is called 'king of the satyrs' and alerted to a threat from Kleon, the demagogue whose career lies principally in the 420s. 'King of the satyrs' alludes intertextually, it is argued, to Kratinos' *Dionysalexandros* with its chorus of satyrs and the allusion by innuendo to Perikles. It is assumed that the two comedies are close in date. Norwood (1931: 123–4) dated Kratinos' *Dionysalexandros* to the Lenaia of 430 and Hermippos' comedy to the Dionysia of the same year.

Certain of the details related in the hypothesis are seen to apply not just generally to Perikles (see below), but specifically to his career around 430: Athene's promise of 'courage in war' (or 'success in war')[15] to discontent in 430 over his conduct of the War (see Thucydides 2.59–65), Rutherford's explanation of 'on the making of sons' as referring to Perikles' legitimation of his son by Aspasia after the death of his other sons in the plague of 430/29, and 'the Greeks burning the land' as inspired by the

---

[13] Eupolis fr. 259, a badly mutilated papyrus commentary to his *Prospaltioi*, suggests that Eupolis addressed the spectators at the opening of that comedy also. See Storey (2003: 232–3).

[14] Geissler (1969: ix, 24–5) favours 430 or 429, but canvasses other suggestions. Luppe (1966: 182), Rosen (1987: 53), and Revermann (1997) all prefer 430. Norwood (1931: 123–4), followed by Schwarze (1971: 21–4), puts *Dionysalexandros* at the Lenaia of 430. Flickinger (1910) thought that 'the war' was the Spartan invasion of 446 and dated the comedy to 445.

[15] The papyrus has ευφυχι, which Grenfell and Hunt (1904: 71) expanded to εὐτυχίας ('success'), Austin (1983: 140) to εὐψυχίας ('courage').

Peloponnesian invasion of 431. All of these details combine to yield the accepted date of 430 or 429.

But must 'the war' indicate the Peloponnesian War? Luppe (1966: 182 n. 1) thought so: 'mit τὸν πόλεμον kann natürlich nur der peloponnesische Krieg gemeint sein', but there is another conflict from the 430s called a *polemos* by both Thucydides (1.115.2) and Plutarch (*Perikles* 25.1), the war following the revolt of Samos from the Athenian *arche* in 440. Plutarch further records (24.1, 25.1) that Perikles was attacked publicly for getting Athens involved in what began as a conflict between Samos and Miletos in order to gratify Aspasia, his Milesian mistress. I argue in Storey (2005a forthcoming) that this reflects a campaign in both tragedy and comedy by which the war with Samos is recast in terms of the Trojan War, and that one such comedy was Kratinos' Dionysalexandros. Mattingly (1977), arguing that 'the war' was in fact the Samian War, proposed a date of 439. He called attention to the decree 'μὴ κωμῳδεῖν', passed in 440/39 and repealed in 437/6 (Σ *Ach.* 67), which must mean a ban on personal humour (τὸ ὀνομαστὶ κωμῳδεῖν) rather than on comedy itself,[16] and infers from the comment in the hypothesis 'through innuendo' that Kratinos had to resort to innuendo because of the ban on open personal attack.

Mattingly preferred a date of 439, early in the life of the decree, but I prefer 437 or 436 for two reasons. First, Euripides' produced his controversial *Telephos* in 438, a play about a Greek war in Asia fought for a woman, whose production in the aftermath of the Samian War and its attendant controversy adds a significant level of meaning. If *Telephos* does resonate with the campaign at Samos, then the Athenians and Perikles lie behind the Argives and the sons of Atreus (Aspasia being Helen, of course), a natural enough 'equation'. But the representation of Perikles by Alexandros turns him and the Athenians into Trojans, a less natural 'equation', and one that I suggest should be later than *Telephos* (438).

Second, there is Euripides' infamous *Alkestis* in 438, produced in the fourth position (that of satyr-play), but without satyrs. Marshall (2000: 237) has made the attractive suggestion that Kallias' satyrs were comedy's response to the pointed absence of satyrs from Euripides' *Alkestis* in 438. If my date of 437 for *Dionysalexandros* is correct, then two comic poets

---

[16] *IG Urb. Rom.* 216.4 shows that Kallias' comedy, *Satyroi*, was produced in 437.

were commenting pointedly on the satyrs missing from Euripides' drama the previous year.[17]

The points in the hypothesis mentioned above that might be thought to apply to Perikles do not necessarily compel a date in 430 or 429. For instance, as for 'courage' or 'success in war', Plutarch (*Perikles* 18) records an instance of Perikles' military caution in the 440s. A reference in comedy to his shortcomings as a military leader does not necessarily belong in 430. Similarly 'begetting of sons', even if that were the reading of the mysterious and abbreviated text in line 8, could surely have a meaning other than Perikles' legitimation of his son by Aspasia. I will concede that 'ravage the country' does certainly fit the circumstances of the Spartan invasions of 431 and 430, although Thucydides II uses τέμνειν and δῃοῦν for the ravaging of Attica, rather than πυρπολεῖν. But is this one detail enough to fix the comedy in 430 or 429? Luppe (1966: 182–4) thought so, but once we have entertained the possibility that another conflict lies behind the 'war' of the hypothesis, we must wonder if a reference to the Greeks 'burning the countryside' might not just be a general reference to the conduct of war, rather than to a specific event. If produced the year after *Telephos*, which concerned the Greeks' initial moves into the region surrounding Troy, this might be all that the allusion entailed.

Thus a date of 437 or 436 allows *Dionysalexandros* to become part of a campaign in drama that represented the Samian War in terms of the mythical war between the Greeks and the Trojans, a campaign that will also have involved Euripides' lost *Telephos*, and perhaps even Sophokles' *Antigone* as well.[18] If Hermippos fr. 47 (Perikles addressed as 'king of the satyrs') does allude intertextually to the chorus of Kratinos' comedy, the allusion can be one over a number of years (six or seven by my estimation). It also reveals that both tragic and comic dramatists could use

---

[17]Ekphantides' *Satyroi* may also belong to the 430s. His début belongs to 457–455 (*IG* ii2 2325.49, between Euphronios in 458 and Kratinos in 454), but fr. 5 makes fun of Androkles, a *komodoumenos* of the 430s and 420s. If fr. 5 comes from his *Satyroi*, then a third comedian could have been taking Euripides to task for the missing Satyrs.

[18] Lewis (1988) dates *Antigone* to 438 and sees in the non-burial of Polyneikes an allusion to the story related in Plutarch (*Perikles* 28.2) of the mistreatment of the Samian dead.

the events and experiences of a contemporary conflict to 'back up' their dramatic creations, before Aristophanes and Euripides used the Peloponnesian War to 'back up' their plays of the last three decades of the fifth century.

## *Perikles and the Comedy*

Clearly if it were not for the throw-away comment by the author of the hypothesis, 'in the play Perikles was very convincingly made fun of by innuendo for having brought the war on the Athenians', we would not have suspected that this essentially mythological burlesque possessed any contemporary relevance. But the writer's comment raises a host of questions:

(a)    Exactly what was the innuendo (*emphasis*)? Was it carried by a subtlety in the words of the play, in the same way that Kleon becomes Paphlagon and Hyperbolos becomes Marikas? Or was it carried, as Revermann (1997) suggests, by a visual cue, in his view the presentation of Dionysos with the distinctively shaped head of Perikles?

(b)    How did the author of the hypothesis know about the innuendo, if it depended on something subtle in the text, or especially if it was carried visually?

(c)    Should we trust the author of the hypothesis? Is the innuendo something that was readily apparent from a reading of the comedy, or is it the product of an overly ingenious Alexandrian scholar's imagination?

(d)    Why did Kratinos have to resort to innuendo? Why not just attack Perikles directly, as he does elsewhere? [This question may be answered if we date the comedy to the period of the 'Morychides decree' (439–436).]

(e)    What was so 'persuasive' or 'effective' about the innuendo that the author of the hypothesis felt compelled to comment upon it?

(f)    Is the reference to Perikles carried by the character of Dionysos or by that of Alexandros?

Critics from Croiset onwards (1904: 308) assume that Perikles' involvement in the comedy is through the character of Dionysos – 'C'est donc bien celui-ci [Dionysos] qui représentait Periclès'. Schwarze (1971: 6–24), Revermann (1997), and McGlew (2002: 46–56) provide perhaps the most blatant statements of the interpretation that Dionysos is everywhere a hostile caricature of Perikles. For Revermann the principal character of the comedy is a 'fusion of political and mythical identity, a Διονυσπερικλεαλέξανδρος'. For McGlew (2002: 46–56) the comic portrait explores the dichotomy between Perikles' public self-picture of personal abnegation and his gratification in private of his personal appetites. On his reading Kratinos has transformed 'the famous Judgement of Paris into a comic Judgment of Pericles' (2002: 48).

The hypothesis is then subjected to a minute analysis in a search for details that might apply allegorically to Perikles. To this end the gifts of the goddess have been seen as possessing a particular appropriateness for Perikles: that of Hera, 'unshaken tyranny' – which Perikles could be seen to possess, that of Athene, 'courage in war' – which he allegedly did not,[19] and that of Aphrodite (whatever we read in the text) referring to his supposed sexual propensity and affair with Aspasia. Dionysos as judge of the contest reflects Perikles' power to decide for peace or war, his fear of the Greeks (lines 30–3) an allusion to Perikles' unpopularity for the conduct of the War, and the surrender of Dionysos to the Greeks (especially the Spartan Menelaos) a comic reflection of the Spartans' demand for the banishment of Perikles as one of 'the accused' (Thucydides 1.126–7). Aspasia becomes Helen, the bringer of war, for which see also Eupolis fr. 267.[20] We may add Rutherford's (1904) interpretation of 'on the begetting of sons' as an allusion to Perikles' legitimation of his son by Aspasia. Flickinger (1910: 9) saw in fr. 42 ('do you want door-posts and decorated porches') a critique of Perikles' grand building policy.

But was this comedy a full-length political allegory, behind which Dionysos is always to be seen as representing Perikles,[21] or was the

---

[19] Rosen (1988: 52), reading εὐτυχίας here, sees a parallel in Perikles' prayer at Thucydides 2.13.2.

[20] McGlew (2002: 49), however, thinks that Kratinos meant the satyrs, notoriously lascivious creatures, to represent Aspasia.

[21] Rosen (1988: 52) sums up the *opinio communis* well: 'after seven decades of scholarship on this issue, however, there is little doubt that the whole play can be construed as an allegorical attack on Pericles'. Even Heath (1990: 147) departs from his usual

'innuendo' introduced at just one moment in the comedy, in a choral song or a parabasis, or even visually as Revermann suggests? Körte (1904: 491), followed by Norwood (1931: 118–24), thought that the play was essentially a burlesque of myth and not a political comedy of the sort that we know from Aristophanes, and I would tend to agree. The various points of contact mentioned above may be just coincidences and the product of ingenious imagination – after all, the specific promises of the goddesses were part of the established myth – as at *Trojan Women* 923–30. In particular, 'tyranny' was the standard word for 'kingship' in Greek drama, especially in Sophokles, where no pejorative force is intended, and also at *Trojan Women* 928 in this exact context. The re-emergence of 'tyranny' as an emotive word in Athenian politics belongs to the late 420s and 410s, not to the early 430s.[22]

Must the innuendo depend on an equation throughout between Dionysos and Perikles? I suspect that the critics have been too eager to regard the comedy as more than a burlesque of myth and to see the presence of Perikles in the character of Dionysos and the events of the drama. Could the subtle implication have been created by an equation between Perikles and Alexandros? If I am right about the early date for the comedy and about the sub-text of the Samian War, then the point of the similarity is that Perikles (Alexandros) was seduced by the attraction of a woman (Helen/Aspasia) into bringing Athens (Greece) into a war in the eastern Aegean. The widening of the comedy to include Perikles will then have come at the end of the comedy, perhaps in a choral song at the close of the play, when Alexandros was on stage. I might entertain a variation of Revermann's theory that the innuendo was a visual cue, but it was Alexandros who entered with headgear that would suggest Perikles – either the elongated helmet or possibly a Phrygian cap designed to resemble the infamous Odeion of Perikles. After all in another fragment of Kratinos Perikles is described as:

---

caution, 'the Greek invasion and Dionysus' cowardly reaction to it could make an excellent satire on Pericles' defensive strategy'.

[22] For the 420s see *Wasps* 461–525, where Bdelykleon says at lines 490–1, 'I haven't heard the word [*tyrannis*] for over fifty years, and now it is as common as salted-fish'; for the 410s see the attacks on Alkibiades for aiming at a tyranny (Thucydides 6.18).

> Here comes Perikles, the onion-headed Zeus, wearing the Odeion on his
> head now that the *ostrakon* is gone (fr. 73 – *Thrattai*).

A coin with a rough sketch of the Odeion, found in Judeich (1931: figure
38),[23] looks for all the world like a raised cap, and if Alexandros entered so
costumed, the innuendo at Perikles could be carried by this visual cue and
perhaps something in the text to equate Helen with Aspasia. Again, if
*Dionysalexandros* belongs in the aftermath of Samos, the relationship
between Perikles, Aspasia, and an eastern war works well. There is no
need to assume that the subtle thrust at Perikles was carried by the figure
of Dionysos throughout; we should consider seriously whether the
innuendo was worked around the appearance of Alexandros. The comedy
was known as 'Dionysalexandros', and I suspect that Körte and Norwood
were correct to regard the principal theme of the comedy as a mythological
burlesque of the story of Alexandros. I have long been tempted by van
Leeuwen's emendation of δι' ἐμφάσεως to δι' Ἀσπασίαν. If correct, then an
earlier date for the comedy seems a much better proposition, since we
know from Plutarch that Perikles was attacked in the early 430s for getting
Athens involved in the Samian War to gratify Aspasia.

## The identity of the chorus

On the surface there should be no problem here. At lines 6–12 a plural
group ('these') address the spectators 'about the begetting of sons' (or
'about the poets') and subsequently laugh at Dionysos when he appears.
Later in the hypothesis (lines 42–44) we hear of 'the satyrs encouraging
him [Dionysos] and promising not to betray him'. The natural assumption
is that both plurals refer to the same group, a collection of satyrs who
formed the chorus of the comedy. Dionysos is, of course, associated with
satyrs, especially in the satyr-drama, and jeering and joking (as at lines 11–
12) would suit such a chorus well.

Not all have agreed, however. Luppe (1966: 185–7) concluded from
'Alexandros … orders <them> to take them [Dionysos and Helen] to the
ships, to hand them over' (lines 34–7)' that the satyrs would be an unlikely

---

[23] An illustration of this coin accompanied Revermann's initial presentation of his
theory about *Dionysalexandros*, at the Rivals of Aristophanes conference in 1996.

group to hand over Dionysos, especially as they will later promise (lines 43–4) not to desert him. In his view the actual chorus of the comedy was composed of Alexandros' fellow-shepherds. He followed Edmonds (1957: 32) in regarding the second line of the superscription at the top of column ii: ΔΙΟΝΥϹ[ΑΛΕΞΑΝΔΡΟϹ / Η [ /] ΚΡΑΤ[ΕΙΝΟΥ] as indicating an alternative title ('*Dionys[alexandros* / or [ / ] of Krat[inos]'). For this he suggested Kratinos' *Idaioi* ('Men of Ida' – compare line 23). Fr. 90 of that lost comedy is attested by Σ *Thesm.* 215 as the original of the shaving scene in that comedy. Fr. 91 mentions 'divine shapes appearing at the beginning', which might allude to the appearance of the goddesses. Fr. 39 was seen as further evidence:

> And here inside are shearing knives, with which we trim the sheep and the shepherds.

The 'we' would be Luppe's shepherds explaining their way of life to an ignorant Dionysos.[24] Heath (1990: 46–7) suggested Kratinos' *Dionysoi* as the alternative title, on the basis of fr. 52 ('may he win who speaks what is best for the city'), which he thought fit well with a discussions 'to the spectators about the poets'.[25] The problem is that *Dionysalexandros* is a comedy with double identities, but it is Alexandros of whom there are two, not Dionysos.

Schmid (1946: 77 n. 8) and Rosen (1988: 55 n. 59) both found joking at Dionysos inappropriate for a chorus of satyrs, supposedly supporters and friends of the god – Rosen in particular sees in the verbs ἐπισκώπτουσι and χλευάζουσιν not just mild banter but 'genuine invective'. If the 'real' chorus were composed of Trojan shepherds, these might be expected to react with derision at the appearance of Dionysos disguised inappropriately.

However, I find these arguments unconvincing. Luppe was concerned that the satyrs would not be the appropriate ones to hand over Dionysos and Helen, but why should it be the chorus who effect the transfer?

---

[24] Schmid (1946: 77 n. 8) had earlier argued that there were two choruses in the comedy, one of satyrs and the other of shepherds, the latter being the οὗτοι of line 6. Luppe (1966: 185–7) did not commit himself to the identity of the οὗτοι; either shepherds or satyrs in his view could jeer at Dionysos.

[25] Only one fragment of *Dionysoi* survives, fr. 52 cited in the *Lexicon Messanense*. Was this a mistaken citation of *Dionysalexandros*?

Alexandros could just as easily have ordered an attendant or perhaps a fellow-shepherd or two to take them into custody, just as the Proboulos in *Lysistrate* is accompanied by some Scythian archers (line 434), so also the Prytanis at *Thesmophoriazousai* 929ff. Much of the support for a chorus of shepherds comes from fr. 39, which in Luppe's view is spoken by a chorus of shepherds explaining their life to Dionysos. But it seems to me that it could equally well belong to Dionysos upon his return with Helen to Ida (line 23), when she is confronted with the stark realities of life with a shepherd-prince in the wild. Frr. 42 and 43 may also belong to such a scene. Croiset (1904) thought that these fragments came from an early scene with the goddesses distressed at the humble surroundings, Körte (1904) and others reasonably saw Dionysos as the addressee faced with the prospect of a shepherd's life. An even more likely setting would be Dionysos/Alexandros acquainting Helen with the realities of her new life – see fr. 39 above. Fr. 43 could be part of Helen's sarcastic reply. Kock (1880: 24) regarded Alexandros as the subject of fr. 43, whose life as a prince is at odds with his life as a shepherd.

Rosen laid considerable stress on the verbs in the hypothesis, ἐπισκώπτειν and χλευάζειν, concluding that these suggest sustained and hostile invective, rather than mild banter. Both verbs occur again at *Frogs* 375–6, part of the parodos of that comedy, in which incidentally the chorus 'talks to the audience about poets' and indulges in mocking and insult. Despite the connotations for χλευάζειν, which Rosen draws from later sources, its use at *Frogs* 375–6 is essentially mild, part of ritual insult rather than any sustained hostility. Even the jokes at Archedemos *et al.* at *Frogs* 416ff. seem more funny than serious, and I would see a less forceful significance in the verb and conclude that the chorus of satyrs make fun of Dionysos when he returns dressed as a shepherd. This is precisely what Herakles does at *Frogs* 42ff., when he views Dionysos wearing the odd combination of the lion-skin and *krokotos*, and the relative of Euripides at the sight of the gender-challenged Agathon at *Thesmophoriazousai* 130–45.

Satyrs, then, seem to be the most likely group to have formed the chorus of this comedy. Satyrs belong naturally to the realm of satyr-play; indeed they are the *sine qua non* of that dramatic genre. But they occur also in comedy. We can detect as many as nine comedies from the period 486–323 with a chorus of satyrs.[26]

## *'Dionysos as anti-hero'*

So Alan Sommerstein (1996: 11) aptly describes this repeated theme in Old Comedy. Drama was produced at the festivals of Dionysos, and whether we accept an origin within the worship of Dionysos or not, he was the principal deity of the occasion.[27] But tragedies about Dionysos and his myths are not that common, and he and his retinue of satyrs are much more frequently found in satyr-drama. Similarly he appears often in comedy. For the fifth and early fourth century we know of two comedies called 'Dionysos' by Magnes (distinguished as 'first' and 'second' at Athenaios 367f, 646e), a *Dionysoi* by Kratinos (if this is in fact a separate comedy from *Dionysalexandros*), a *Dionysos Asketes* ('Dionysos in Training') by Aristomenes, a *Dionysos Nauagos* by Archippos or Aristophanes, a *Dionysou Gonai* ('Birth of Dionysos') by Polyzelos, and Demetrios' *Dionysou* [..., where the editors of *POxy*. 2659 have restored another *Dionysou Gonai*. He appeared also as the main character in Aristophanes' *Frogs*, similarly in his *Babylonians*, as the unlikely naval recruit in Eupolis' *Taxiarchoi*, a character in Ameipsias' *Apokottabizontes*, and as the speaker of Hermippos fr. 77.

The comic picture of Dionysos consists of a combination of humorous stereotypes, some of which are shared by tragedy and satyr-play as well: (i) Dionysos as luxury-loving and uncourageous – *Frogs* 116–35, 279–311, 464–502, 738–40; Eupolis frr. 271–3, 280; Hermippos fr. 77; (ii) Dionysos in an incongruous situation where he performs badly and ludicrously – *Frogs* 59–115, 805–13; fr. 75 (*Babylonians*); Eupolis' *Taxiarchoi*; Aristomenes' *Dionysos Asketes*; Archippos' or Aristophanes' *Dionysos Nauagos*; (iii) Dionysos in disguise – *Frogs* 45–8, 494–674; Eupolis frr. 272–3; *Thesm.* 130–45 (a comic parody of Aeschylus' *Edonians*); (iv) the penetration of that disguise and a debate over his identity – *Frogs* 494–674, and (v) the physical indignities (or threat

---

[26] I study this matter more fully in Storey (2005b forthcoming).

[27] For a vigorous assault on the traditional view that tragedy originated from the rituals of Dionysos see Scullion (2002).

thereof) inflicted on Dionysos during the action – *Frogs* 197–268, 605–74; Eupolis frr. 268.48–55, 270, 275, 277–8.

Kratinos' comedy seems to have employed all of these motifs. First fr. 40 presents him in his traditional guise ('*thyrsos*, saffron-robe, quite elaborate, drinking-cup'). In fr. 41, ('as soon as you heard my [their, his] words, you started grinding your teeth'), if the 'you' grinding his teeth is Dionysos in distress, then he displayed his cowardly reaction to a threatening situation. This situation could be either the advent of the goddesses or (more plausibly) the entrance of an understandably annoyed Alexandros. Second his substitution for Alexandros as judge of a divine beauty contest certainly qualifies as an incongruous situation. If in fr. 42 Dionysos is the one who wants 'porches and decorated door-posts', then the luxury-loving Dionysos has found himself very much out of his element. Third Dionysos changes his appearance and identity twice in the comedy, becoming first a Trojan shepherd and then a ram. Fourth he successfully maintains his fictitious role as Alexandros, fooling both the Greeks and Helen, but his disguise is easily penetrated by Alexandros (lines 33–5 of the hypothesis).[28] Fifth and finally, Alexandros 'sends Dionysos away to be handed over' (lines 40–1). The actual discovery of Dionysos may well have been accompanied by a scene of physical violence (or threat thereof), as at *Frogs* 464–502, 605–73. Thus Kratinos seems to have been working well within the traditional framework for the presentation of Dionysos in comedy. In tragedy Dionysos seems to have triumphed over his adversaries (*Lykourgos*, *Pentheus*). In comedy his success is not necessarily assured. In Eupolis' *Taxiarchoi* it is a reasonable assumption that Dionysos rose above his bumbling attempts at military training and ended up on top, in *Frogs* he returns with Aeschylus to 'save the city', in *Babylonians* he encounters a demagogue (fr. 75) and in light of Kleon's subsequent anger we can assume that Dionysos got the best of that figure. But in Kratinos' comedy he is handed over to the Greeks for whatever horrible fate awaits him.

---

[28] We can confidently assign fr. 45 ('and the silly fool wanders about like a sheep, going "baa, baa" ') to this scene; the speaker is very likely to have been Alexandros.

## *Conclusions*

My reading of the hypothesis and the admittedly scanty fragments of this intriguing lost comedy suggests the following conclusions:

(a)   A date of 437 for the play should be seriously entertained, within the period of the decree μὴ κωμῳδεῖν and in the aftermath of the Samian War, which would be 'the war' mentioned in the last line of the hypothesis.

(b)   The chorus of the comedy was made of the satyrs who regularly accompany Dionysos, and there is no need to regard the satyrs as a sub-chorus (perhaps mute) and to postulate a 'real' chorus made up of Alexandros' fellow-shepherds. If the comedy does belong in 437, then it, like Kallias' *Satyroi*, may well have been pointedly commenting on the absence of satyrs from Euripides' *Alkestis* in 438.

(c)   Not much has been lost before the hypothesis becomes intelligible, perhaps one or two short scenes where Hermes enlists Dionysos to serve as judge of goddesses.

(d)   Lines 7–9 record an address by the chorus 'to the spectators', most likely 'concerning the poets'. Here Kratinos breaks the dramatic illusion in the manner of an Aristophanic parabasis, but in *Dionysalexandros* this occurs much earlier than in Aristophanes, perhaps in the parados of the comedy. The formal parabasis will have come during Dionysos' absence in Greece to collect Helen (lines 20–1).

(e)   If we may trust the author of the hypothesis, at some point in the comedy Perikles was attacked 'by innuendo' for 'having brought the war upon the Athenians'. But we should not assume that this comedy contained a play-length allegory with Perikles lying beneath Dionysos throughout. The point of the comparison may have lain with Alexandros rather than with Dionysos.

I have called attention earlier to the parodos of *Frogs*, where the anapaests that one would expect in a parabasis show up much earlier at lines 354–71. Here the chorus is in fact speaking 'to the spectators concerning the poets', including among the 'cursed' those who do not appreciate good comedy. The scenes that immediately follow the parodos will contain much humour directed against Dionysos and others. In the song that follows these anapaests (372–416) the chorus use the same verbs ἐπισκώπτειν and χλευάζειν (375–6) as used in the hypothesis, and at 417–40 engage in some formal abuse at Archedemos, Kallias, and Kleisthenes. Earlier in the anapaests (357) Kratinos is mentioned by name – those who have 'not been initiated into the rites of bull-eating tongue of Kratinos' should leave immediately – and I wonder if this parodos with its words 'concerning the poets', followed by laughing and jeering at Dionysos and others, is something of an intertextual homage to Kratinos' earlier comedy, which, like *Frogs*, is a play about a disguised Dionysos judging a contest.

# How Aristophanes got his A&P[1]

## *Alan H. Sommerstein*

(University of Nottingham)

I never planned to create an edition of the eleven comedies of Aristophanes. As an undergraduate, I planned to take two years of the Classical Tripos, then change to Law and make that my profession. But my Director of Studies at King's, Patrick Wilkinson, wasn't having any of that, and I had to admit that there was something to be said for not leaving a field in which I was doing rather well. And then there began to happen a series of accidents.

For the second part of the Tripos I was concentrating on what was called, as it still is, "Group E" – linguistics and comparative philology – and after graduating in 1968 I moved immediately into doctoral research in this area: Cambridge had no Master's courses in these days, and an MA still arrived automatically three years after the BA. My intention was to spend a year in America, getting acquainted with linguistics somewhere near the cutting edge, and then return to get on with my thesis. Here befell the first accident. In the summer of 1968 I visited Rome on a travel exhibition, naively choosing the worst possible time of year to go there; soon after my return I fell ill and was diagnosed with hepatitis, most probably caused by the tasty but perhaps inadequately washed salads of which I had freely partaken. That put America out of consideration for the time being, and I returned to King's.

Sir Frank Adcock, co-editor and guiding spirit of the original *Cambridge Ancient History*, ran a Greek play-reading circle in the college – though "play" was an elastic term, and included from time to time an

---

[1] I deeply appreciate the honour done me by John Rich in organizing the colloquium to mark the completion of my series of Aristophanic editions, of which this volume is the result. The present article is contributed to it at his suggestion.

adaptation of the *Iliad* with a favoured undergraduate in the role of narrator, or, to use Adcock's term, of "wapthode". Adcock had died on 22 February 1968, a few hours after the circle had met to read Aristophanes' *Clouds*. I am fairly sure that it was in preparation for that meeting that I had bought the edition of the play by Kenneth Dover, which had then just appeared – an edition that can fairly be said to have been epoch-making for Aristophanic studies. I had taken very little interest in Aristophanes as an undergraduate, and had attended no lectures on him; Dover began to help me see what I was missing. After Adcock's death, the other members of the play-reading circle decided to continue its activities, which were now hosted by the musician (and former classicist) Philip Radcliffe. In the autumn, however, a reading of Aristophanes' *Thesmophoriazusae* had to be abandoned half-way, because the participants were helpless with laughter. I had always been addicted to comedy in its more modern forms; an author who was as funny as this had to be worth further investigation. But my course was already set, my English-Speaking Union fellowship awaiting its holder. In January 1969, at the start of the spring semester, I set off for frosty Indiana, to sit at the feet of ... well, actually nobody in particular, since the big-name professors hardly ever taught; but I got into the swim of the subject, at least as far as phonology (the study of the sound systems of languages) was concerned, and had on the whole an enjoyable six or seven months before the *Queen Elizabeth II* brought me back to Southampton in August.

I naturally returned to Cambridge, and then followed another accident. In late October 1969 I was in Heffers bookshop; I remember I was contemplating a book called *Dionysus: A Social History of the Wine Vine* (by Edward Hyams, I now discover) when my eye fell on an Aristophanes volume in the Penguin Classics series. I bought it for five shillings, took it back to King's, opened it, and was hooked. It was by David Barrett (not that the name then meant anything to me), it contained *Wasps, Thesmo-phoriazusae* and *Frogs*, and it was sheer joy the whole way through. I was not in a position to judge the translator's scholarship, knowing so little of the subject myself, but it was obvious that he had loved every minute of his work, and he was able to communicate his enthusiasm to this reader at least. Eleven years later, with an echo of Keats that still expresses my feelings, I wrote of the spirit which, speaking out loud and bold, taught me how intensely Aristophanes was to be enjoyed, and impelled me to do what I could to help others to enjoy him also.[2]

Long before I reached the end of the book, I was wondering why there was nothing else like it. Of course I had come across other translations of Aristophanes; they were mostly in verse and rather dull (and, as I was to discover, incomplete). Even the still classic versions of Benjamin Bickley Rogers, lively and ingenious as they were, were somewhat restricted by their verse form; like Barrett, I thought that for a translation of a comedy to work, especially with an author whose comic effects depend on the moment rather than the sustained situation, the spoken parts had to be rendered in prose (though not, of course, prosily).

Now I had always enjoyed translating from and into Latin and Greek, and had even once tried my hand at creating a translation of a Roman comedy (but soon found that Terence didn't appeal to me). And so it was that instead of being a good boy and getting on with my thesis, I chose a new trio of plays and set to work on translating them. I chose *Clouds* because of Dover's edition (then still unique), *Acharnians* because it was the play I had enjoyed most at school, and *Lysistrata* because it was new to me and seemed very well structured. I went off at a great lick and soon had *Clouds* complete, but I got bogged down with *Acharnians*. This was to some extent Rogers' fault: I was working mainly from his edition (which was as good as any then available) and often found it difficult to improve on his renderings.

At this point my recollections become a bit vague, probably because they are intertwined with other events that caused me some distress, but so far as I can recall, things happened like this. I had a girlfriend, an undergraduate (not a classicist); we'll call her C. She happened to look through my translation of *Clouds*, and rather liked it. In March 1970 I was elected a fellow of King's. The next day C told me that she had definitely transferred her affections to another student. It would be pointless to cloak *him* in anonymity, since I have named him elsewhere in print; he was David Watkinson, now a barrister of considerable note. Several months later, I learned that he had seen my translation and thought I ought to try and get it published; I think this information must have come to me

---

[2] *Aristophanes; Acharnians* (Warminster, 1980), vi.

through a friend of C's, whom I cultivated for nearly a year in the hope that she might become a conduit for a renewal of contact with C. (She could not, alas, herself become a successor to C, since she was a lesbian. Or at least that's what she told me.)

At that time, in the winter of 1970/71, I was concentrating on my thesis, *Phonological Theory and Ancient Greek*, which was completed soon afterwards and examined in May 1971.[3] But it was again an event in my emotional life that brought a new turn to the story of my relations with Aristophanes: my engagement in mid-March to Rebecca Hardoon (we married at the end of August). This seems to have been the stimulus I needed to get me back to the project, and somehow, too, I was now able to use Rogers without being dependent on him. I completed *Acharnians* and *Lysistrata* in a few months – I remember being anxious to polish *Lysistrata* off before the wedding date. There must have been some revision to follow, since it was not till 26 November that, taking David Watkinson at his word so to speak, I sent the three plays to Penguin.

Had I known anything of publishers, I would not have been surprised to hear nothing for seven weeks; but I didn't, and I was. Possibly, however, I had merely addressed my parcel to the wrong person. On 14 January 1972 one of Penguin's editors, Julia Vellacott, wrote expressing some interest, though noting that they had an overlapping volume already under contract; this turned out to be by David Barrett himself, and within two weeks agreement had been reached between Barrett, myself, and Betty Radice, editor of the Penguin Classics, that my volume should appear first and I should then collaborate with Barrett on a further volume which would include the five Aristophanic plays not yet covered. *Lysistrata and Other Plays* (Penguin's title – it had not occurred to me that *Lysistrata* was the plum of the volume from the marketing point of view) was published late in 1973; it was completely devoid of scholarly value, I have consistently warned my students not to use it, and up to the end of 2002 (when it was replaced by what was called a "revised edition" but was really a complete rewrite) it had sold 316,646 copies (not counting the miniature version of *Lysistrata* alone that was published as part of Penguin's diamond jubilee

---

[3] A revised version of part of the thesis was published by the Philological Society as *The Sound Pattern of Ancient Greek* in 1973.

celebrations in 1995). *The Birds and Other Plays,* produced jointly with Barrett, followed in 1978.

At this point the Loeb Classical Library comes into the story. This great institution had had bad luck with Aristophanes.[4] John Williams White – teacher and friend of James Loeb, and emeritus professor of Greek at Harvard – had been an obvious choice to edit and translate the comedies for the series when it was founded in 1911. He was one of the outstanding Aristophanic scholars of his day, author of the first comprehensive survey of Aristophanic manuscripts (*CP* 1 [1906] 1–20, 255–278), and soon to produce the first edition of Aristophanic scholia to be founded on satisfactory critical principles (*The Scholia on the Aves of Aristophanes* [Boston, 1914]) and a major study of comic metre (*The Verse of Greek Comedy* [London, 1912]); he was, moreover, in the process of preparing a monumental critical edition of the whole eleven comedies. However, he died in 1917 leaving apparently nothing in a publishable state,[5] and the series editors (T. E. Page, W. H. D. Rouse and Edward Capps) eventually decided to make use of Rogers' version, supplying some sections of *Lysistrata* and *Thesmophoriazusae* which Rogers had forborne to translate,[6] and providing annotation (on the limited Loeb scale) and some very skimpy introductions derived, with drastic abridgment, from Rogers'

---

[4] So, curiously, has that other great institution, the Oxford Classical Texts series, which for a century has been defiled by the edition of Hall and Geldart (1900–1, 2nd ed. 1906–7), on which Gelzer (*RE* Suppl. XII [1971], 1419) says all that is necessary: "Handschriften schlecht referiert, unkritischer Text." It is good to know that the new OCT of Nigel Wilson is only a few months away.

[5] Except for collations of the manuscripts of *Wasps* and *Birds* and analyses of the textual traditions of these plays; these studies, carried out together with Earnest Cary, were published in *Harvard Studies in Classical Philology* 29 (1918), 77–131 and 30 (1919), 1–35.

[6] *Lysistrata* 904–967, 985–992, 1088–96, 1099; *Thesmophoriazusae* 635–643. The reader is informed that these passages were not included in Rogers' version, but is not told to whom the published translations of them are due. Other passages bowdlerized by Rogers are left as he wrote them; sometimes the actual meaning of the Greek is elucidated by a footnoted Latin translation, sometimes by a note *in Greek* (a method Rogers had himself used in his commentaries), and sometimes an omission or loose paraphrase is let pass without any warning or explanation at all. The actual translations show all Rogers' usual dexterity, and are remarkably faithful to the Greek, given the constraints under which he had to work; but he was fully conscious of their inadequacies and, departing from his usual practice, had printed them following, not facing, the Greek text.

editions. This hybrid, published in 1924 (under the sole name of Rogers, who had died five years earlier), represented Aristophanes in the Loeb series, most inadequately, for (as it turned out) three-quarters of a century; it was the only complete edition of Aristophanes since 1868 that went unmentioned in Thomas Gelzer's comprehensive 1971 *RE* article on the poet (*RE* Suppl. XII 1391–1570), which recorded every one of Rogers' editions of individual plays.

Betty Radice was herself a contributor to the Loeb series, having published in 1969 a two-volume edition of the letters of the younger Pliny (together with his panegyric on Trajan) based on her Penguin translation of six years earlier, and it was on her suggestion that on 25 April 1972 I approached the series editor, E. H. Warmington, with a proposal for a new Loeb Aristophanes. He replied on 22 May, in a letter which marks the true commencement of the edition that was completed thirty-one years later. He was unsure whether it would be best to have a "revised Rogers" or an entirely new translation, but in any case a revised Greek text and "some sort of critical apparatus" would be necessary, as would "new introductions and bibliography"; at any rate,

> I would like one person to do the whole, and that man would appear to be you, and I am approaching no other.

Warmington must surely have taken some advice before entrusting so weighty a project to a 24–year-old junior research fellow with no scholarly track record at all in the relevant subject area, but I have never discovered whose it was.

It was soon agreed that the translations should be new: if, as all concerned agreed, the Rogers translation was (in Warmington's phrase) "a work of literature in its own right", it made no sense to destroy its integrity by posthumous revision. Since my intention at that time was to base the Loeb translations on the Penguin ones, I was anxious for Barrett to take part in the project, and this was agreed to during 1973. The text, apparatus, notes and introductions would be my responsibility, but Barrett would supply revisions of his existing or forthcoming Penguin translations (to be vetted for accuracy by me) for *Wasps, Birds, Thesmophoriazusae, Frogs* and *Ecclesiazusae*, and both names would appear on the title-page. I set to work forthwith, drafting a provisional apparatus and reading the secondary literature.

All this time, though I was doing some invited lecturing for the Faculty of Classics and a considerable amount of undergraduate supervision for King's and other colleges, I still regarded myself, and was regarded, as primarily a theoretical linguist; I was publishing articles like "On the so-called definite article in English" and "The margins of morpho-phonemics"[7] in the *Journal of Linguistics* and *Linguistic Inquiry,*[8] I was under contract to write a textbook on phonological theory for the publisher Edward Arnold, and I was a member of the King's College Research Centre project on theoretical linguistics along with such current and future luminaries as P. H. Matthews and Bernard Comrie. The Loeb, strange as it may seem, had to be regarded as a *parergon.*

Then in December 1973 my application for renewal of my research fellowship (due to expire in September 1974) proved unsuccessful, and I had to look for a job – all the more urgently because Rebecca was expecting our first child in March. I naturally applied for posts in linguistics (including one in Australia), but was only shortlisted once, and was on the point of quitting academia for the civil service. At this stage a vacancy was announced at Nottingham for a specialist in Greek drama. The interviews were scheduled for the day on which the birth was officially due. Rebecca took vigorous and successful measures to persuade Louise to arrive a day early; I went to the interview and got the job. Inevitably it directed my research as well as my teaching interests increasingly away from linguistic theory, but for most of the next three or four years I was still dividing my time about equally between the Loeb and the phonology textbook. I tended to work on the latter on Mondays and

---

[7] For reasons mysterious to me, this article has twice been anthologized in recent years – in J. Goldsmith ed. *Phonological Theory: The Essential Readings* (Oxford, 1999 – extracts only) and in C. W. Kreidler ed. *Phonology* (London, 2000). It originally appeared in *Journal of Linguistics* 11 (1975), 249–259.

[8] The second word of this title should be pronounced like "ink-worry", with the stress on the first syllable. The paper referred to (*Linguistic Inquiry* 3 [1972], 197–209) attempted to demonstrate that the English definite article was "really" a pronoun, in response to an article by Paul Postal (in D. A. Reibel and S. A. Schane ed. *Modern Studies in English* [Englewood Cliffs NJ, 1969], 201–224) which had argued that English pronouns were "really" definite articles; those were the sorts of games that syntactic theorists were playing at the time.

Tuesdays, the former (with, I came to notice, distinctly greater enthusiasm) on Wednesdays and Thursdays. The younger present-day reader will wonder where teaching and administration came into the picture; the answer is that in those days the department's annual student intake was in single figures, and such administrative work as was needed all seemed to be done by one person, Ronnie Watson, without anyone else, including the Head of Department, needing to be much bothered.

After the publication of *Modern Phonology* in 1977, I felt myself played out as a theoretical linguist, though I was still reviewing books on the subject as late as 1985. By now the first volume of the Loeb, comprising four plays, was nearing completion, and in 1978 I was within weeks of submitting it (even the index was ready). Then out of a clear sky there came a thunderbolt from Harvard University Press. A certain Arthur J. Rosenthal, of whom I never heard before or since, informed me that owing to "the financial circumstances of the Library and of scholarly publishing in general" it had become necessary to restrict "the production of new volumes … to a rate of not more than one a year", that it would therefore not be possible to publish my volumes for at least five years, that even after that no guarantee could be given, and that accordingly he was writing "to cancel these volumes". The Loeb Aristophanes had been chopped.[9]

I was, naturally, devastated at this apparent loss of several years' investment of labour, and wrote at once to Eric Handley, then professor of Greek at University College, London, and director of the Institute of Classical Studies. He knew my work well, and in 1977 he had read and commented warmly on my draft introduction for the Loeb. He replied sympathetically, and undertook to explore the possibilities of getting the edition or translation published in some other form, perhaps by the University of London's publishing house, Athlone Press. I had been much impressed by the Prentice-Hall series of translations of Greek tragedy, with

---

[9] I ought to add that, happily, neither my relations with the Loeb Library nor those of Aristophanes were destined to terminate there. A new four-volume Loeb Aristophanes, begun in 1998, was completed in 2002 by Jeffrey Henderson of Boston University, who in the meantime had also succeeded George Goold as series editor, and in the same year I was invited to prepare a two-volume Loeb edition of Aeschylus (replacing the edition of 1922–26 by Herbert Weir Smyth) for delivery in 2007.

introductions and limited, elucidatory annotations, including those of Aeschylus' *Oresteia* by Hugh Lloyd-Jones, of his *Seven against Thebes* by C. M. Dawson, and of Euripides' *Bacchae* by Geoffrey Kirk,[10] and thought that the Loeb material could easily be adapted to a similar format. In May, however, the Athlone Press's board turned down the idea, mainly no doubt because the Press itself was in some difficulty financially.

Neither my records nor my recollection are very clear about what happened next, but I know that both Eric Handley and George Goold, his UCL colleague who was also now the Loeb series editor, played crucial roles. They brought my situation and plans to the attention of John Aris, the founder and senior director of the small specialist publisher Aris & Phillips of Warminster, Wiltshire (and, incidentally, the father and father-in-law of that heroic couple, Michael Aris and Aung San Suu Kyi). I visited his home just off Belgrave Square, and by the early summer of 1979 all was arranged. The intention was to publish the whole edition, one volume to one play (though there was no formal advance commitment, each volume being the subject of a separate contract). There would be a general introduction, an introduction to each play, text, apparatus, a new translation, and annotation (keyed to the translation) on a rather more generous scale than was possible in the Loeb – though I did not then envisage it as constituting a "commentary" in anything like the full sense.[11] I invited David Barrett to contribute as before, but he had already been feeling increasingly reluctant (as he put it in a letter of March 1979) to "marry our 'popular' versions to a scholarly edition of the text", and accordingly, with his blessing, I carried on alone.

*Acharnians* appeared in 1980, to quite a warm critical welcome, and despite a serious illness in 1980–81 (which resisted diagnosis for fifteen months, until surgery revealed it as a benign but intermittently bleeding intestinal tumour) it was quickly followed by *Knights, Clouds* and *Wasps*, which had all been part of the completed Loeb volume. The commentaries were already growing more ambitious, with a broader concept of what called for elucidation and with more argument and referencing – an

---

[10] All these were published in 1970; Lloyd-Jones' *Oresteia* was reissued, with revisions and a new introduction, by Duckworth (London) in 1979, after the Prentice-Hall series had folded.

[11] Indeed, the annotation was first described as a "commentary" on the contents page in *Thesmophoriazusae* (1994), and on the title page not till *Ecclesiazusae* (1998).

evolutionary trend that was to continue incrementally all through the series: whereas *Acharnians* had had 58 pages of annotation, *Wasps*, on a comic text only 25% longer, had 97. The introductory notes to the plays,[12] however, remained brief and, some would say, critically simplistic, and some reviewers rightly complained of the absence of bibliographies to the individual plays, and of indexes. The preface of *Knights* promised "comprehensive indexes ... in the final volume of the series"; in fact there proved to be no room for them there, and they have appeared separately as a twelfth volume. Bibliographies to individual plays were provided as from *Peace* (1985), though their omission from the first four volumes was not made good until the publication of *Addenda* in the eleventh volume, *Wealth* (2001).

Meanwhile, the Aristophanes editions had become the model for something far bigger, for what has come to be known as "the A&P series" of bilingual editions. It started slowly, with editions of Persius by J. R. Jenkinson (1980) and of Lucan VIII by Roland Mayer (1981), but it has grown and grown, and as of today (15 March 2005) there are 23 volumes in print, forthcoming or with a "reprint under consideration", by authors from Homer to Cassius Dio[13] and from Plautus to William of Newburgh (1136–98). No doubt it is my own specialized interests that lead me to draw particular attention to one section of this library. The Euripides series, with Christopher Collard as general editor and an introduction by Shirley Barlow printed in every volume, was begun in 1986 and now comprises fourteen volumes (including one of selected fragmentary plays); it will eventually include all the nineteen plays of Euripides that survive complete and as many more that do not.

Progress with the Aristophanes series inevitably became slower after *Wasps*, since although much preliminary work on the other plays had been done during the seventies, no actual text, translation or notes had yet been created. After *Peace* (1985) and *Birds* (1987) it slowed down further, only one volume appearing in the next six years. This was due to various

---

[12] The term "introductory note" was replaced by "introduction" as from *Frogs* (1996), by when the two or three pages of the early volumes had grown to twenty-three.

[13] *The Augustan Settlement* (Roman History 53–55.9) ed. J. W. Rich (1990).

causes. Student numbers and University bureaucracy were both on the increase. The advent of Research Assessment Exercises meant some deviation of effort into areas which it was thought would score well with assessment panels, such as collaborative activities and international conferences.[14] The replacement of my faithful electric typewriter with its golfball heads, which had been bought for me at the time of my first Aris & Phillips contract and had served me for thirteen years, by a personal computer, though of course it brought vast long-run benefits, in the short run was highly disruptive, particularly since I at first had no Greek font capability (I had to use the Departmental office machine outside office hours) and later only a very primitive system (misnamed Turbofonts) which had a distinct set of keystrokes, often three or four together, for each *combination* of a letter and diacritic(s); it took me two hours to type the first two lines of *Thesmophoriazusae*. During most of 1992 my research activity was at a complete halt; it is doubtless not a coincidence that 1992 was the year in which I became Head of Department for the first time on the retirement of Wolfgang Liebeschuetz, the year in which Nottingham undergraduate courses were modularized, and the year of a Research Assessment Exercise in which I was both mainly responsible for the department's submission and myself a member of the assessment panel.

There are few better restoratives, however, than extended exposure to *Thesmophoriazusae*. I enjoyed working on this play more than on any of its predecessors, and think I may have made a greater original contribution to its detailed understanding than for any other play. For *Frogs* I was able to acquire a Greek font that was much more elegant in appearance and much more user-friendly, and the apparatus (which in *Thesmophoriazusae* had been banished to stand between text and commentary) was able to return to its proper position beneath the text.[15] By now I felt I was on the home stretch of what David Lewis, in a review of *Knights* many years

---

[14] I had never attended a conference outside the UK before 1991 – another fact that may amaze the younger academic reader.

[15] Another innovation in the *Frogs* volume was the inclusion of an updated version of the general Aristophanic bibliography which had appeared in the first volume of the series. How badly the update was needed is shown by the fact that of 63 items (in the *Wealth* volume, in 2001, the list had stretched to 88) in the updated bibliography (excluding editions of text or scholia, and bibliographical surveys) only 27 had figured in the original listings.

before,[16] had called, presumably with a quiet word-play, "the long road to *Wealth*"; but when the practicalities of the *Wealth* volume itself were examined, it became clear that the end of the road had not come yet. *Wealth* is a short play and in some ways quite a simple one – few lyrics, little of Aristophanes' usual verbal razzle-dazzle, relatively little detailed topicality. The commentary would not be overwhelmingly long (though even so, it ran to 83 pages, with more lines to the page than in *Wasps* and with a much smaller font[17]). But I also intended to include in the volume a section of addenda bringing all the previous volumes up to date, and with this added the *Wealth* volume actually became the longest in the series, at 321 pages, and no room was left for the indexes, which it was therefore agreed to publish as a twelfth volume. This volume was sent to Aris & Phillips on 29 August 2002.

Of the five persons who had done most to make it possible for the series to be created, only Eric Handley has lived to see it completed. Betty Radice died in 1985, George Goold in 2001, David Barrett and John Aris both in 1989. Aris's son-in-law Adrian Phillips succeeded him in the leadership of the firm, but in 2002, at the age of sixty, he decided to retire and to sell the firm to David Brown, proprietor of Oxbow Books of Oxford who had for some time acted as Aris & Phillips' distributors. Thus it came about that while the index volume, like its predecessors, appeared under the Aris & Phillips imprint, early in 2003, its official place of publication had moved from Warminster to Oxford. After just under thirty-one years, the project that began with my 1972 letter to E. H. Warmington is at last complete.

At the end of these thirty-one years, I still see Aristophanes much as I saw him at the beginning: a master of verbal and theatrical art, with a sure sense of what would raise a laugh, and ready at any moment to sacrifice almost any other effect for the sake of doing so – but at the same time a man with clear ideas about what was best for his community, many of which were often unpalatable to the majority of his compatriots (though less so, probably, to that skewed sample of them who attended the theatre).

---

[16] *Classical Review* 33 (1983), 175–7.
[17] The longest commentary in the series was that on *Frogs*, which occupied 143 pages and 86,000 words.

I see now more clearly than I did then that many of his ideas (not necessarily, or even usually, the same ones) also are, or should be, unpalatable to us today: to name a few, his eagerness to encourage his audiences to be mirthful at the expense of the sick or handicapped (at least if they were also regarded as despicable for other reasons), his readiness to make peace at almost any price with the brutal and short-sighted oligarchs of Sparta and (as *Birds* shows) to make war at the drop of a hat against almost anyone else, his hostility to institutions (such as the payment of jurors) essential, in Athenian conditions, to the maintenance of an effective democracy.[18] But we must remember that we only know about these things because the particular art-form that Aristophanes practised was one that required him to make his characters speak directly about contentious contemporary issues. Very likely there were painters or sculptors, or even tragic poets, in his day whose social and political attitudes were by our standards even more disagreeable; but *they* were under no obligation to express those attitudes in their work. And at a deeper level Aristophanes offers us a wonderfully positive attitude to life, finely perceived by Michael Silk towards the end (pp.403–9) of his richly suggestive book *Aristophanes and the Definition of Comedy* (Oxford, 2000). I have tried to paraphrase it at the end of the introduction to my revised Penguin translation:[19]

> Nothing is beyond imagination; no one is contemptible (except those who choose to make themselves so); everything that can be seen and felt and experienced is of interest, and capable of generating happiness through laughter; and we are what our past has made us, though our nature also impels us to reach out for an ideal future.

---

[18] I have discussed the issues on which these sentences touch in "How to avoid being a *komodoumenos*", *Classical Quarterly* 46 (1996), 327–356; "The theatre audience and the Demos", in J. A. López Férez ed. *La comedia griega y su influencia en la literatura española* (Madrid, 1998), 43–62; "Comedy and the Unspeakable", in D. L. Cairns and R. A. Knox (eds.) Law, Rhetoric, and Comedy in Classical Athens (Swansea 2004), 205–222; "Harassing the satirist: the alleged attempts to prosecute Aristophanes", in R. M. Rosen and I. Sluiter ed. *Freedom of Speech in Classical Antiquity* (Leiden, 2004), 145–174; and "Alternative democracies and alternatives to democracy in Athenian Old Comedy", to appear in U. Bultrighini ed. *Democrazia e antidemocrazia nel mondo greco*.

[19] *Aristophanes: Lysistrata and Other Plays*[2] (London, 2002), xxxix.

If that credo can be said to be implicit in Aristophanes' text – and like Silk, I think it can – then the study and performance of that text can surely be a force for good, whether or not we are willing to laugh at everything the dramatist invites us to laugh at, and whether or not his vision of an ideal future exactly corresponds to any of ours.

I said above that the project begun in 1972 is now complete. Perhaps not entirely. I am continuing to compile "Addendis addenda", and I think I would like one day, after my retirement, to revise the whole edition into something which would be, if not of course the last word, at any rate *my* last word (more or less) on Aristophanes. I have lived with him too long to part now for ever; I suspect that others would not let me do so if I tried – and anyway, one can be together with him for forty years, or more, and as Rogers and Victor Coulon and Kenneth Dover and many another can testify, it won't seem a day too much.

I wish to end by recording, in alphabetical order, the names of those whose contributions towards making it possible for me to begin and to complete this edition should not in my opinion go uncommemorated. Some of them have already been named above, some in the prefaces of one or more volumes, some have not been explicitly acknowledged before. May the completed work please them, and for those who are no longer here, may it be an honour to their memory.

| | | |
|---|---|---|
| †Sir Frank Adcock | Eric Handley | Jim Roy |
| †John Aris | Jeffrey Henderson | Niall Slater |
| M. Atkinson | Ismene Lada-Richards | †Shirley Smith |
| Colin Austin | Wolfgang Liebeschuetz | Rebecca Sommerstein |
| †David Barrett | Douglas MacDowell | †Theophil Sommerstein |
| David Brown | Toph Marshall | R. L. Tattersall |
| †Helen Butler | Benedetto Marzullo | Pascal Thiercy |
| C | Giuseppe Mastromarco | †Edward Thompson |
| Andrew Crompton | Doug Olson | †Sylvia Warmingham |
| Francesco De Martino | Michael J. Osborne | †E. H. Warmington |
| Greg Dobrov | Franca Perusino | David Watkinson |
| Sir Kenneth Dover | Dawn Petherick | †Ronnie Watson |
| Nan Dunbar | Adrian Phillips | †Patrick Wilkinson |
| Adrienne Edwards | †Philip Radcliffe | Nigel Wilson |
| A. P. Fawcett | †Betty Radice | Bernhard Zimmermann |
| †George Goold | John Rich | |
| Stephen Halliwell | Ralph Rosen | |

# Bibliography

Althusser, L. (1969), *For Marx* (London).

Althusser, L. (1971), *Lenin and Philosophy, and other essays* (London).

Austin, C. (1973), *Comicorum Graecorum fragmenta in papyris reperta* (Berlin/ New York).

Austin, C. and Olson, S. D. (2004), *Aristophanes: Thesmophoriazusae* (Oxford).

Beazley, J. D. (1971), *Paralipomena* (Oxford).

Booth, A. (2002), *What's Left?* (London).

Bowie, A. M. (1993), *Aristophanes. Myth, Ritual and Comedy* (Cambridge).

Bowie, E. L. (1988), 'Who is Dicaeopolis?', *Journal of Hellenic Studies* 108, 183–185.

Brockmann, C. (2003), *Aristophanes und die Freiheit der Komödie: Untersuchungen zu den frühen Stücken unter besonderer Berücksichtigung der Acharner* (Munich/Leipzig).

Calvino, I. (1986), *The Uses of Literature* (New York).

Carpenter, T. H. (1991), *Art and Myth in Ancient Greece* (London).

Coetzee, J. M. (2001), *Stranger Shores: Literary Essays, 1986–1999* (New York).

Croiset, M. (2004), 'Le *Dionysalexandros* de Cratinos', *Revue des études grecques* 17, 297–310.

Csapo, E.G., and W.J. Slater (1995), *The Context of Ancient Drama* (Ann Arbor).

Cusset, C., Carrière, J.-C., Garelli-François, M.-H. and Orfanos, C. (eds.), (2000), *Où courir? Organisation et symbolique de l'espace dans la comédie antique* (*Pallas* 52, Toulouse).

Dale, A. M. (1957), 'An interpretation of Ar. *Vesp.* 136–210 and its consequences for the stage of Aristophanes', *Journal of Hellenic Studies* 77, 205–11, reprinted in *Collected Papers* (Cambridge, 1969), 103–18.

de Ste. Croix, G. E. M. (1972), *The Origins of the Peloponnesian War* (London).

Dearden, C. W. (1976), *The Stage of Aristophanes* (London).

Dover, K. J. (1966), 'The Skene in Aristophanes', *Proceedings of the Cambridge Philological Society* 192, 2–17, reprinted in *Greek and the Greeks* (Oxford, 1987), 249–66.

Dover, K. J. (1968), *Aristophanes: Clouds* (Oxford).

Dover, K. J. (1972), *Aristophanic Comedy* (Berkeley & Los Angeles).

Dover, K. J. (1980), *Plato: Symposium* (Cambridge).

Dover, K. J. (1992), 'The Language of Criticism in Aristophanes' *Frogs*', in B. Zimmermann (ed.), *Antike Dramentheorien und ihre Rezeption* (Stuttgart), 1–13.

Dover, K. J. (1993), *Aristophanes: Frogs* (Oxford).

Edmonds, J. M. (1957), *The Fragments of Attic Comedy*, vol. 1 (Leiden).

Ercolani, A. (2002), 'Sprechende Namen und politische Funktion der Verspottung am Beispiel der *Acharner*', in A. Ercolani (ed.), *Spoudaiogeloion. Form und Funktion der Verspottung in der aristophanischen Komödie* (Stuttgart/ Weimar), 225–254.

Flashar, H. (1967), 'Zur Eigenart des Aristophanischen Spätwerkes', *Poetica* 1, 154–75, English version ('The Originality of Aristophanes' Last Plays') in E. Segal (ed.) *Oxford Readings in Aristophanes* (Oxford, 1996), 314–28.

Foley, H. P. (1982), 'The "Female Intruder" Reconsidered', *Classical Philology* 77, 1–21.

Foley, H. P. (1988), 'Tragedy and Politics in Aristophanes' *Acharnians*', *Journal of Hellenic Studies* 108, 33–47.

Ford, A. (2003), 'From Letters to Literature: Reading the 'Song Culture' of Classical Greece' in Yunis (2003), 15–37.

Freud, S. (1905/1960), *Jokes and their Relation to the Unconscious* (tr. J. Strachey) (London).

Geissler, P. (1969), *Chronologie der altattischen Komödie*, 2nd ed. (Dublin/ Zurich).

Gratwick, A. S. (1993), *Plautus: Menaechmi* (Cambridge).

Grauert, W. H. (1828), 'De mediae Graecorum comoediae natura et forma', *Rheinisches Museum* 2, 62.

Grenfell, B. P. and Hunt, A. S. (1904), 'Argument of Cratinus' ΔΙΟΝΥCΑΛΕΞΑΝΔΡΟC', *The Oxyrhynchus Papyris*, vol. IV (London).

Grethlein, J. (2003), *Asyl und Athen. Die Konstruktion kollektiver Identität in der griechischen Tragödie* (Stuttgart/Weimar).

Halliwell, S. (1984), 'Aristophanic Satire', *The Yearbook of English Studies* 14, 6–20.

Handley, E. W. (1993), 'Aristophanes and his theatre', in J. M. Bremer and E. W. Handley (eds.), *Aristophane* (Entretiens Hardt 38, Geneva), 97–123.

Heath, M. (1990), 'Aristophanes and his Rivals', *Greece & Rome* 37, 143–58.

Heberlein, F. (1981), 'Zur Ironie in "Plutos" des Aristophanes', *Würzburger Jahrbücher für die Altertumswissenschaft* 7, 27–49.

Heitsch, E. (2002), *Apologie des Sokrates* (Platon. Werke I 2) (Göttingen).

Henderson, J. (1991), *The Maculate Muse. Obscene Language in Attic Comedy*, 2nd ed. (New York/Oxford).

Herington, C. J. (1985), *Poetry Into Drama: Early Tragedy and the Greek Poetic Tradition* (Berkeley and London).

Hubbard, T. K (1991), *The Mask of Comedy. Aristophanes and the Intertextual Parabasis*. (Ithaca/London).

Imperio, O. (1998), 'La figura dell'intellettuale nella commedia greca', in A. M. Belardinelli *et al.* (eds.), *Tessere. Frammenti della commedia greca. Studi e commenti* (Bari), 43–130.

Issacharoff, M. (1987), 'Comic space', in J. Redmond (ed.), *Themes in Drama* 9: *The Theatrical Space* (Cambridge).

Jauss, H. R. (1982), *Ästhetische Erfahrung und literarische Hermeneutik* (Frankfurt/Main).

Kaibel, G. (1895), 'Kratinos' Ὀδυσσεύς und Euripides' Κύκλωψ', *Hermes* 33, 82–5.

Kassel, R. and Austin, C. (1983), *Poetae Comici Graeci*, vol. IV (Berlin/ New York).

Koch, K. D. (1968), *Kritische Idee und komisches Thema. Untersuchungen zur Dramaturgie und zum Ethos der Aristophanischen Komödie*, 2nd ed. (Bremen).

Kock, T. (1880), *Comicorum Atticorum Fragmenta*, vol. I (Leipzig).

Konstan, D. (1990), 'A City in the Air: Aristophanes' *Birds*', *Arethusa* 23, 183–207.

Körte, A. (1904), 'Die Hypothese zu Kratinos' *Dionysalexandros*', *Hermes* 39, 491–8.

Laclau, E., & Mouffe, C. (2001), *Hegemony and Socialist Strategy: Towards a Radical Democratic Politics*, 2nd ed. (London).

Lewis, R. G. (1988), 'An alternative date for *Antigone*', *Greek, Roman, and Byzantine Studies* 29, 35–50.

Lowe, N. J. (1988), 'Greek stagecraft and Aristophanes', in J. Redmond (ed.), *Themes in Drama* 10: *Farce* (Cambridge), 33–52.

Luppe, W. (1966), 'Die Hypothese zu Kratinos' *Dionysalexandros*', *Philologus* 110, 169–93.

Luppe, W. (1980), 'Nochmals zum Paris-Urteil bei Kratinos', *Philologus* 124, 154–8.

Luppe, W. (1988), 'ΠΕΡΙ ῩΩΝ ΠΟΙΣΕѠС,' *Zeitschrift für Papyrologie und Epigraphik* 72, 37–8.

Macherey, P. (1978), *A Theory of Literary Production* (London).

Marshall, C. W. (2000), '*Alcestis* and the problem of prosatyric drama', *Classical Journal* 95, 229–38.

Mattingly, H. (1977), 'Poets and Politicians in Fifth-Century Greece', in K. H. Kinzl (ed.), *Greece and the Eastern Mediterranean in Ancient History and Philosophy* (Berlin/ New York), 231–45.

McGlew, J. (1997), 'After Irony: Aristophanes' *Wealth* and its modern interpreters', *American Journal of Philology* 118, 35–53.

McGlew, J. (2002), *Citizens on Stage: Comedy and Political Culture in the Athenian Democracy* (Ann Arbor).

Meineke, A. (1839), *Fragmenta Comicorum Graecorum* (Berlin).

Möllendorff, P. von (1995), *Grundlagen einer Ästhetik der Alten Komödie: Untersuchungen zu Aristophanes und Michail Bachtin* (Classica Monacensia 9, Tübingen).

Muecke, F. (1982), 'A Portrait of the Artist as a Young Woman', *Classical Quarterly* 32, 41–55.

Ober, J. (1999), *Political Dissent in Democratic Athens: Intellectual Critics of Popular Rule* (Princeton).

Olson, S. D. (1988), 'The "Love Duet" in Aristophanes' *Ecclesiazusae*', *Classical Quarterly* 38, 328–330.

Olson, S. D. (1990), 'Economics and Ideology in Aristophanes' *Wealth*', *Harvard Studies in Classical Philology* 93, 223–42.

Olson, S. D. (2002), *Aristophanes: Acharnians* (Oxford).

Parker, L. P. E. (1991), 'Eupolis or Dicaeopolis?', *Journal of Hellenic Studies* 111, 203–8.

Perdrizet, P. (1905), 'Hypothèse sur la première partie du "Dionysalexandros" de Cratine', *Revue des études anciennes* 7, 109–115.

Poe, J. P. (1999), 'Entrances, Exits, and the Structure of Aristophanic Comedy', *Hermes* 127, 189–207.

Poe, J. P. (2000), 'Multiplicity, discontinuity, and visual meaning in Aristophanic Comedy', *Rheinisches Museum* 143, 256–295.

Pöhlmann, E. (1988), *Beiträge zur antiken und neueren Musikgeschichte* (Frankfurt).

Pöhlmann, E. (1995), 'Aristophanes auf der Bühne des 5. Jh.', in id. (ed.), *Studien zur Bühnendichtung und zum Theaterbau der Antike* (Studien zur klassischen Philologie 93, Frankfurt), 133–42.

Prato, C. (ed.) (2001), *Aristofane: Le Donne alle Tesmoforie* (Milan).

Rau, P. (1967), *Paratragodia. Untersuchung einer komischen Form des Aristophanes* (Munich).

Reinders, P. (2001), *Demos Pyknites. Untersuchungen zur Darstellung des Demos in der Alten Komödie* (Stuttgart/Weimar).

Revermann, M. (1997), 'Cratinus' Διονυσαλέξανδρος and the head of Pericles', *Journal of Hellenic Studies* 117, 197–200.

Rogers, B. B. (ed.) (1907), *The Plutus of Aristophanes* (London).

Rosen, R. M. (1988), *Old Comedy and the Iambographic Tradition* (Atlanta).

Rosen, R. M. (1997), 'Performance and Textuality in Aristophanes' *Clouds*', *Yale Journal of Criticism* 10.2, 397–421.

Ross, K. (1996), *Black and White Media: Black Images in Popular Film and Television* (Oxford).

Rothwell, K. S. (1990), *Politics and Persuasion in Aristophanes' Ecclesiazusae, Mnemosyne* Supplement, vol. 111 (Leiden).

Ruffell, I. A. (2000), 'The World Turned Upside Down: Utopia and Utopianism in the Fragments of Old Comedy', in D. Harvey and J. Wilkins (eds.), *The Rivals of Aristophanes: Studies in Athenian Old Comedy* (London), 473–506.

Ruffell, I. A. (2002), Review of Alan H. Sommerstein (ed.), Aristophanes: *Wealth, Bryn Mawr Classical Review* 2002.08.43, http://ccat.sas.upenn.edu/bmcr/2002/2002–08–43.html (visited 13/05/03).

Rutherford, W. G. (1904), 'The date of the *Dionysalexander*', *Classical Review* 18, 440.

Russo, C. F. (1961), *Aristofane autore di teatro* (Florence); expanded 1984, 1992; further expanded & translated as *Aristophanes, An Author for the Stage* (London & New York, 1994).

Schmitt-Pantel, P. (1992), *La cité au banquet* (Rome/Paris).

Schwinge, E.-R. (1977), 'Aristophanes und die Utopie', *Würzburger Jahrbücher für die Altertumswissenschaft* 3, 43–67.

Scullion, S. (2002), '"Nothing to do with Dionysus": tragedy misconceived as ritual', *Classical Quarterly* 52, 102–37.

Silk, M. (1990), 'The People of Aristophanes', in C. B. R. Pelling (ed.), *Characterization and Individuality in Greek Literature* (Oxford), 150–173.

Slater, N. W. (2002), *Spectator Politics: Metatheatre and Performance in Aristophanes* (Philadelphia).

Sommerstein, A. H. (1980), *The Comedies of Aristophanes. Vol. 1: Acharnians* (Warminster).

Sommerstein, A. H. (1981), *The Comedies of Aristophanes. Vol. 2: Knights* (Warminster).

Sommerstein, A. H. (1982), *The Comedies of Aristophanes. Vol. 3: Clouds* (Warminster).

Sommerstein, A. H. (1983), *The Comedies of Aristophanes. Vol. 4: Wasps* (Warminster).

Sommerstein, A. H. (1984), 'Aristophanes and the Demon Poverty', *Classical Quarterly* 34, 314–333.

Sommerstein, A. H. (1985), *The Comedies of Aristophanes. Vol. 5: Peace* (Warminster).

Sommerstein, A. H. (1987), *The Comedies of Aristophanes. Vol. 6: Birds* (Warminster).

Sommerstein, A. H. (1989), *Aeschylus: Eumenides* (Cambridge).

Sommerstein, A. H. (1990), *The Comedies of Aristophanes. Vol. 7: Lysistrata* (Warminster).

Sommerstein, A. H. (1992), 'Old Comedians on Old Comedy', in B. Zimmermann (ed.), *Antike Dramentheorien und ihre Rezeption* (Stuttgart), 14–33.

Sommerstein, A. H. (1994), *The Comedies of Aristophanes. Vol. 8: Thesmophoriazusae* (Warminster).

Sommerstein, A. H. (1996a), *The Comedies of Aristophanes. Vol. 9: Frogs* (Warminster).

Sommerstein, A. H. (1996b), 'How to Avoid Being a *Komodoumenos*', *Classical Quarterly* N.S. 46, 327–356.

Sommerstein, A. H. (1998), *The Comedies of Aristophanes. Vol. 10: Ecclesiazusae* (Warminster).

Sommerstein, A. H. (2001), *The Comedies of Aristophanes. Vol. 11: Wealth* (Warminster).

Sommerstein, A. H. (2002a), *The Comedies of Aristophanes. Vol. 12: Indexes* (Oxford).

Sommerstein, A. H. (2002b), 'Die Komödie und das 'Unsagbare'', in A. Ercolani (ed.), *Spoudaiogeloion. Form und Funktion der Verspottung in der aristophanischen Komödie* (Stuttgart/Weimar), 125–145. (English version, 'Comedy and the Unspeakable', in D. L. Cairns and R. A. Knox (eds.), *Law, Rhetoric and Comedy in Classical Athens* (Swansea, 2004).)

Sourvinou-Inwood, C. (1989), 'Assumptions and the Creation of Meaning: Reading Sophocles' *Antigone*', *Journal of Hellenic Studies* 109, 134–148.

Stevens, P. T. (1956), 'Euripides and the Athenians', *Journal of Hellenic Studies* 76, 87–94.

Stohn, G. (1993), 'Zur Agathonszene in den *Thesmophoriazusen* des Aristophanes', *Hermes* 121, 196–205.

Storey, I. C. (1990), 'Dating and Re-dating Eupolis', *Phoenix* 44, 1–28.

Storey, I. C. (2002), 'Cutting Comedies', in J. Barsby (ed.), *Greek and Roman Drama: Translation and Performance*, *Drama* 12 (Stuttgart), 146–67.

Storey, I. C. (2003) *Eupolis, Poet of Old Comedy* (Oxford).

Storey, I. C. (2004) 'The Curious Matter of the Lenaia Festival of 422', in D. Phillips and D. Pritchard (eds.), *Sport and Festival in the Greek World* (London), 281–92.

Storey, I. C. (2005a– forthcoming), 'Euripides, Comedy, and the War(s)', in F. Muecke, J. Davidson, and P. Wilson (eds.), *Greek Drama III*, *BICS* Supplement (London).

Storey, I. C. (2005b–forthcoming), 'But Comedy has satyrs too', in G. Harrison and J. Francis (eds.), *Tragedy at Play* (London).

Taaffe, L. K. (1993), *Aristophanes and Women* (London/New York).

Taplin, O. (1993), *Comic Angels and Other Approaches to Greek Drama Through Vase-Painting* (Oxford).

Taylor, C. C. W. (1995), 'Politics', in J. Barnes (ed.), *The Cambridge Companion to Aristotle* (Cambridge).

Thieme, G. (1908), *Quaestionum comicarum ad Periclem pertinentium capita tria* (Leipzig).

Thiercy, P. (1986), *Aristophane: Fiction et dramaturgie* (Paris).

Thiercy, P. (2000), 'L'Unité de lieu chez Aristophane', *Pallas* 54, 15–23.

Thomas, R. (1992), *Literacy and Orality in Ancient Greece* (Cambridge).

Thomas, R. (2003), 'Prose Performance Texts: *Epideixis* and Written Publication in the Late Fifth and Early Fourth Centuries', in Yunis (2003), 162–88.

Ussher, R. G. (1973), *Aristophanes, Ecclesiazusae* (Oxford).

van Leeuwen, J. (1904), 'ad Cratinum', *Mnemosyne* 32, 406.

Vidal-Naquet, P. (1986), 'Slavery and the Rule of Women in Myth, Tradition and Utopia', in *The Black Hunter: Forms of Thought and Forms of Society in the Ancient World* (Baltimore), 205–223.

Wiles, D. (1997), *Tragedy in Athens: Performance Space and Theatrical Meaning* (Cambridge).

Wiles, D. (2000), *Greek Theatre Performance: An Introduction* (Cambridge).

Yunis, H. (ed.) (2003), *Written Texts and the Rise of Literate Culture in Ancient Greece* (Cambridge).

Zimmermann, B. (1983), 'Utopisches und Utopie in den Komödien des Aristophanes', *Würzburger Jahrbücher für die Altertumswissenschaft* 9, 57–77.

Zimmermann, B. (1992a), 'Hippokratisches in den Komödien des Aristophanes', in J. A. López Férez (ed.), *Actas del VIIe colloque international hippocratique* (Madrid), 513–525.

Zimmermann, B. (1992b), 'Comedy's Criticism of Music', in N. W. Slater and B. Zimmermann (eds.), *Intertextualität in der griechisch-römischen Komödie* (Stuttgart), 39–50.

Zimmermann, B. (1993), 'Aristophanes und die Intellektuellen', in J. M. Bremer and E. W. Handley (eds.), *Aristophane. Entretiens sur l'antiquité classique* (Vandoeuvres/Genève), 255–286.

Zimmermann, B. (1997), 'Parodie dithyrambischer Dichtung in den Komödien des Aristophanes', in P. Thiercy and M. Menu (eds.), *Aristophane: La langue, la scène, la cité* (Bari), 87–93.

Zimmermann, B. (1998), *Die griechische Komödie* (Düsseldorf/Zürich).

Zimmermann, B. (2000), *Europa und die griechische Tragödie. Vom kultischen Spiel zum Theater der Gegenwart* (Frankfurt am Main).

Žižek, S. (1989), *The Sublime Object of Ideology* (London).